global

expressions

Decorating With Fabrics From Around The World

lisa shepard

Published by

krause publications

700 East State Street • Iola, WI 54990-0001

Please call or write for our free catalog of publications. Our toll-free number to place an order or obtain a free catalog is (800) 258-0929.

Library of Congress Catalog Number: 2001091074
ISBN: 0-87349-290-0

Some products in this book are registered trademarks: Photo Flow™, Fuse-A-Shade™, Liqui-Fuse™, RIT®, Tintex™, and Marble Thix™.

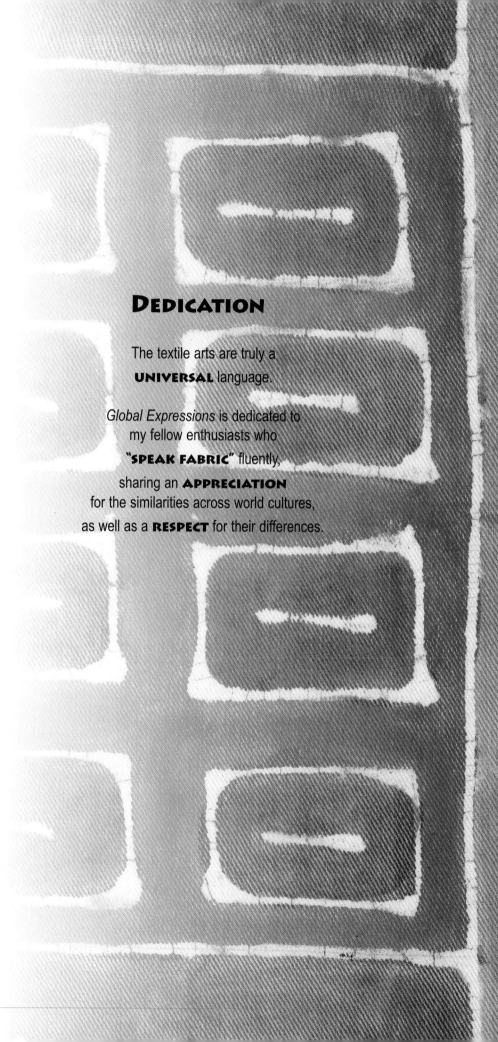

DEDICATION

The textile arts are truly a
UNIVERSAL language.

Global Expressions is dedicated to
my fellow enthusiasts who
"SPEAK FABRIC" fluently,
sharing an **APPRECIATION**
for the similarities across world cultures,
as well as a **RESPECT** for their differences.

TABLE OF CONTENTS

ACKNOWLEDGMENTS

Many people were involved in the process of taking *Global Expressions* from a concept to a reality. In particular, I would like to thank:

Vandarra Robbins, a good friend and a true citizen of the world, for her boundless enthusiasm and all-around assistance with this project.

Edmund Herman of Umoja Photography (www.umojaphoto.com), whose *kuumba* is truly inspiring, and Dawn Niles, for her positive spirit and cross-cultural vision.

iju designs for its excellent on-location services.

My family, especially Sylvia and LeRoy Shepard, for being supportive and for making themselves available in every possible way, and other relatives and friends, who haven't heard from me in months. . .

The companies that have shared their creative passions, their tips and techniques, and their products: Beacon Adhesives/Signature Crafts; Delta Technical Coatings; Exotic Prints; Eastwind Art; HTC, Inc.; Home Arts; International Fabric Collection; Liquitex Artist Materials; Marbled Fabrics; Marcus Brothers Textiles Inc.; Monotapu.com; Novica.com; Putnam; Shambakodzi Crafts; Speedball Art; Trans-Pacific Textiles, Ltd.; Viking Sewing Machine; and Zimports.

My editor, Maria Turner, and the staff at Krause Publications.

Everyone at Marcus Brothers Textiles, for their inspiration and encouragement. You kids are the best!

Thanks also to Exotic Prints, Novica.com, Eastwind Arts, Malcolm Finaulahi Dreaneen, and Cultured Expressions for graciously providing additional photography.

And, for their various contributions to this book, and to my work overall: The African Art Museum of the SMA Fathers, Marjorie Lee Bevis, Jean Biddick, Djema Imports, E'dee Eubank-Robinson, Kerr Grabowski, Karlton J. Herman, Ady Jensen, Kaarta Imports, Kenneth Kweku, Nina Luttinger, Mollin Madziwa, Joanne Newcomb, the Nubian Heritage Quilters' Guild, Carol Peckham, Catherine Ryan, Nidhi Seth, and Herman Smalls.

INTRODUCTION

Today more than ever, our ability to explore the world's cultures continues to grow. Increased international travel and cross-continent relocation, the Internet, and fast-paced communications enable us to learn about, borrow from, and exchange with any other region of the world with ease, even as armchair tourists. It's exciting to think of the possibilities for personalizing these experiences, by bringing globally diverse artifacts directly into our living spaces.

All of this exposure brings us an ever-deepening pool of cross-cultural resources from which to draw, giving rise to an entirely new category in home décor known as "Global Eclectic." This blending and integration of different influences is highly individualized because you're not depending on one particular style. Instead, each piece is deliberately chosen for what it contributes to the whole look: its colors, patterns, textures, fibers, symbolism, and other design elements.

Fiber arts have a way of defining a people like no other art form. On a most basic level, we use fabric in its many forms to protect our bodies from nature's elements, to provide warmth and comfort, and to perform various other functions in our daily lives. So it's not surprising that even the most creative or elaborate textile techniques around the world came about through a combination of necessity and resourcefulness, further developing into the indigenous art forms we appreciate today. Fabrics created for kings and peasants alike are equally marvelous in the eyes of a true international "fabricholic," and each has its own story, its own unique appeal. Fabrics can convey a people's history, traditions, and spiritual beliefs, or they may simply clue us into their daily lives.

You can sew and craft your way around the world by incorporating an international array of specialty fabrics into your decorating scheme. Indonesian hand-dyed batiks used for quilts, dolls, and throw pillows, Japanese sashiko-stitched placemats, or a magazine holder made of sadza fabric from Zimbabwe are all great accents that are sure to spark conversation!

In researching the fabric techniques for this book, I've experienced firsthand the wealth of fabrics, information, and inspiration that's now, quite literally, at our fingertips. I hope you'll be motivated to immerse yourself in the cultures of the world, adapting their traditions and creative talents to fit your own home and your lifestyle.

LISA SHEPARD
www.CulturedExpressions.com

Photo by Cultured Expressions/Courtesy St. Theresa Textile Trove

ABOUT THIS BOOK

GLOBAL EXPRESSIONS is designed to be an introductory look at selected fabric techniques that represent various regions of the world. In compiling the final list of featured fabrics and cultures, I often found similar techniques in other areas. Though the fabrics or processes have different names, it was interesting to consider these comparisons as cultural bridges among the people who created them, whether it was a particular stitch, symbol, or printing process. Where possible, I've attempted to point out such similarities.

For collectors, it might be fun to use these similarities as the basis for a specific collection, such as a grouping of fabrics decorated with stamped motifs that might include Indian block-printed fabrics, adinkra stamping from Ghana, and potato-print fabrics from Zimbabwe. Batik is another fabric craft with many variations worldwide, as is the use of indigo pigment.

To make different fabric styles work together in your projects, look for common elements among them, like a particular color scheme or print motif, as well as interesting contrasts (smooth Indian satin embroideries paired with coarse textures like mudcloth from Mali).

When it comes to putting together a creative atmosphere in your home, optimizing the positive energies of global traditions is becoming a favorite option. It's easy to mix design elements of your own heritage with other cultures for a look that's a distinctive reflection of your personality.

The book is designed to offer a range of ideas for both the fabrics and the home décor pieces; these serve as just the beginning of your decorating "journey," where fabrics and project ideas can be easily interchanged to fit your needs and your favorite fabrics. Beyond the specific projects given, you'll find ideas for other ways to use the fabrics, and these can—and should—also be adjusted to suit your own style.

I always encourage the use of the authentic, imported textiles as much as possible, preferably from one's own world travels, and an interesting piece of fabric (or five or six!) is my souvenir of choice when I travel. As an alternative, special finds acquired through the travels of friends and relatives, coupled with online shopping excursions and local sources, can be equally fruitful in the development of your textile collection. In some cases, these genuine artifacts are more expensive and/or more difficult to find. But remember that eclectic decorating is a gratifying process that evolves over time, so it's not necessary to purchase all of your fabrics or other pieces all at once.

For most of the fabrics, tips and guidelines are included for creating one's own version of a particular fabric. This allows you to enjoy the *influence* of a particular culture, while letting you customize colors, sizes, and other elements to suit your own décor. In either case, the resource listings will be helpful in locating what you need, including source listings for more in-depth study and inspiration. Designers, importers and other resources mentioned within the main chapters are also listed in an appendix at the back of the book.

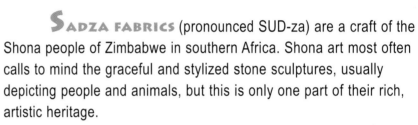

CHAPTER 1

SADZA BATIK
(ZIMBABWE)

SADZA FABRICS (pronounced SUD-za) are a craft of the Shona people of Zimbabwe in southern Africa. Shona art most often calls to mind the graceful and stylized stone sculptures, usually depicting people and animals, but this is only one part of their rich, artistic heritage.

Sadza batiks employ a method of resist, where part of the fabric is masked off, color is applied to other areas, then the masked areas are uncovered to show the design. However, unlike most methods that use wax as a resist, sadza artists use cornmeal instead. In fact, the word "sadza" actually refers to the finely ground maize, or corn, that has long been a staple of the Zimbabwe diet, whether eaten plain or as a side dish. This exemplifies a common theme among world textile arts; that of using what is most accessible in a creative fashion.

The designs found in sadza painted fabrics are traditional geometric patterns, skillfully combined with stylized objects of every-day life. Often these dramatic looks are done in a single color story. This makes it easy to select a sadza to fit your décor. "Earth" tones feature browns, olives, and tans, while various shades of blue represent the "water" colors. "Fire" is depicted in sadza designs of yellows, oranges, and reds, like the sofa covering on page 85.

"Colors also symbolize the rich fruits derived from our natural resources, such as the brown soil, the green leaves, and golden corn," explains sadza artist Mollin Madziwa. "This simplicity of design allows the various color combinations to take center stage, creating striking effects."

Madziwa is also the owner of Shambakodzi, a fair trade organization based in Zimbabwe. Shambakodzi supports, and is supported by, local artisans and skilled-crafts cooperatives, emphasizing the need for the craftspeople to elevate their means of living. In Zimbabwe, the official unemployment figures hover at 70 percent, but this doesn't account for the thousands of Zimbabweans engaged in self-employment through such outlets as Shambokodzi. Their entrepreneurial efforts have enabled the artists to educate their children, build their own homes, and even employ younger people in apprentice-type roles. The organization's success is due in part to their continued cultivation of buyers in the overseas markets. The company was started in 1994, and it also represents craftspeople in the fields of basketry, pottery, metal work, and stone carving.

Most sadza paintings are worked on white or unbleached pure cotton canvas or twill. Sadza artists use cornmeal that is cooked until it is the consistency of mashed potatoes, applying it to the cloth areas that will remain white. These areas usually outline other areas that are later filled with natural dyes.

The fabric, complete with cornmeal outlining, is dried in the sun. Once colors are applied, the cloth is again dried in the sun, and then washed to remove the cornmeal resist.

The craft of sadza batik is mainly a women's activity, and women do crafts to sustain their families while keeping conventional cultural expressions alive and thriving.

Generally, shapes and motifs are fairly simple, including triangles, squares, dots, zigzags, and other universal geometrics, along with simplified animal and human figures. Sadza batik symbols usually tell the story of village life in Zimbabwe and also depict wild animals found in Zimbabwe.

Along with the basic sadza resist technique, many batik artists are also skilled in the creation of potato-stamped designs. Sometimes, the two methods are used on the same piece of fabric, interpreted in a contemporary style. Designs are carved into slabs of potato, and colors are custom-blended for each cloth.

Photo courtesy Novica.com

Tsitsi Zireki is a potato stamp artist with Kudhinda. Sometimes, more than 900 different stamps are used in a single cloth.

Kudhinda Fabrics is another Zimbabwe-based artist cooperative, and potato-print fabrics are a specialty there. New designs are cut daily, to ensure both individuality of each piece and the highest quality printed image; a single cloth might contain more than 900 stamps. These intricate combinations are sometimes used afterwards as the basis for screen-printed versions of their textiles, adding to the versatility and practicality of the original stamped fabrics.

Kudhinda was founded by Zimbabwe native Ros Byrne, whose goal was to redirect the efforts of young graduates facing a bleak job market, steering them toward a more creative and rewarding work enterprise. Kudhinda is represented, in part, by Novica.com, a fine arts and home décor Web site that is dedicated to promoting world artisans and increasing international appreciation for traditional cultures and art forms.

Handpainted fabrics from Zimbabwe have exciting possibilities for home décor, like these earth-toned bedroom coordinates.

Silkscreen designs, like this one being completed by Freeborn Sigauka, another Kudhinda artist, give extended life to the original potato stamp designs.

Decorating With Sadza Batik

My first "sadza sighting" was in 1996, and I bought the piece immediately because it spoke to me. I had to have it, even though it wasn't until a couple of years later that I learned the name and some background on the fabric.

When a fabric, or any decorative piece, affects you like that, it's a feeling you have to go with, regardless of whether you've worked out exactly where to place it in your home at the time. This is especially true if you're visiting a faraway place and the opportunity is unlikely to present itself again. A piece that is truly special to you will always find a place in your home.

Sadza cloths are often designed as smaller separate blocks within complete panels, allowing you to cut the cloth to showcase certain sections as a pillow top, or to use it whole for the most dramatic effect possible.

At Shambakodzi, suggestions for end use of the cloths include clothing, duvet covers, wall hangings, sofa throws, curtains, cushions, and tablecloths.

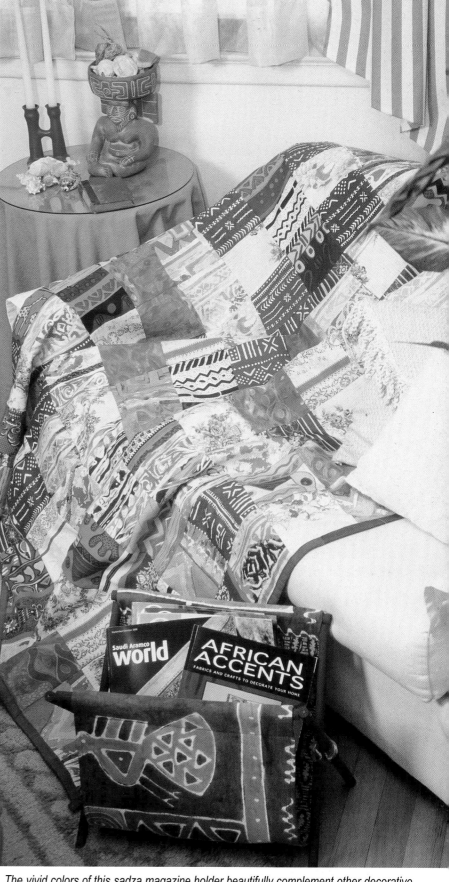

The vivid colors of this sadza magazine holder beautifully complement other decorative accents in a cozy sitting area.

Try Sadza Batik!

Recreate the look of sadza cloth with cornmeal, heavy cotton fabric, and acrylic fabric pints.

You'll Need:

* heavy cotton fabric, ivory or white
* acrylic paints
* fine ground cornmeal*
* containers and stirrers to custom-blend colors (optional)
* reclosable plastic bag (sandwich size)
* textile medium
* paint brushes

*I found some variations in the recipes for the sadza resist. The majority called for finely ground cornmeal as discussed above, however, another version described a paste of plain flour and water, <u>uncooked</u>. The active ingredient in any case is the starch. For my projects, I used cornmeal.

1 Mix equal parts of cornmeal and boiling water in a saucepan. Heat over a low light, stirring constantly to prevent sticking and to work out any lumps. After about one minute, your mixture should have the consistency of smooth mashed potatoes. Set aside.

2 Meanwhile, draw the design on the fabric. In planning your design, remember that the sadza resist should not be placed directly <u>on</u> these lines, since the lines will be visible once the sadza is removed. (Instead, you'll want to apply the sadza just outside or inside any drawn lines, so that the paints will cover these lines.) Be sure your pattern is graphic—the bolder, the better!

3 Spoon the sadza into a reclosable plastic bag, squeezing out all of the excess air before sealing the bag. Cut a small opening in the corner of the bag. Outline the drawn designs with the sadza mixture. Let dry thoroughly for several hours.

4 Prepare paints by adding a textile medium, if desired, following the manufacturer's instructions. This will give the cloth an added measure of washability and light-fastness. Depending on your intended end-use for the cloth, this may or may not be necessary. Paint designs as drawn. Allow to dry thoroughly.

5 Crack off the dried sadza with your hands or a blunt instrument, to reveal the masked areas of the design.

It's easy to apply the sadza (cornmeal) using a reclosable plastic bag.

Once paints are applied, let dry thoroughly, and then crack off the sadza to reveal the designs.

This chessboard is a functional and eye-catching accessory—and a great gift idea for your favorite chess player.

Sadza Chessboard

Apply these bold designs to a custom-made chessboard that does double duty as a great accent for a coffee table or dining area. The easy alternating checkered design is bordered by typical geometric motifs found in traditional sadza.

1 Center craft backing over the wrong side of the cotton fabric, so that the fabric extends about ½-inch all around. Fuse, following the manufacturer's instructions.

2 Place plywood on top of the fused fabric, with the fused side up. Turn one edge of the fabric up over the board and secure with glue or fusible hem tape. Turn under and hem the opposite side, then hem the two remaining sides in the same manner.

3 On the underside of the board, center the backing fabric over the top fabric, covering all raw edges of the top fabric. Glue or fuse backing fabric to the board.

4 On the top of the board, draw a ¼-inch border around all sides.

5 Draw another square 2 inches in from the first. (This will measure about 13½ inches across.)

You'll Need:

- ⅜-inch thick plywood, 18 inches square
- fabric for bottom of the board, 17½ inches square
- fusible craft interfacing, 19 inches square
- fabric glue or fusible hem tape
- cotton fabric for sadza painting, at least 20 inches square
- remaining sadza supplies as noted on previous page
- round wooden beads or ball feet: four medium (1 inch) or twelve small (½-inch)
- short nails or wood glue

6 Divide the inner square into eight boxes vertically and eight boxes horizontally. Remember to draw the lines, just to the left or right of the actual edge of each box, so these lines won't be seen when the sadza is removed. Each of the sixty-four boxes should measure approximately 1⅝ inches.

7 Draw the random designs along the 2-inch-wide border.

8 Following the sadza instructions on the previous page, apply sadza, then color, to the chessboard.

9 When completely dried, remove the sadza resist.

10 Attach the ball feet with small nails or wood glue. If the feet are small, as shown in the sample, use three at each corner. If the feet are larger, one in each corner will be enough. You can also use the felt-covered furniture protectors to finish your board.

A sadza-decorated chessboard even makes a wonderful table accent for decorative candles or a floral arrangement.

SADZA MAGAZINE HOLDER

Keep books, magazines, TV remotes, even needlecrafts handy yet orderly with this colorful, compact organizer. It's the perfect piece to place right near the sofa or by your favorite easy chair.

Sadza cloths are usually sectioned off into separate designs; careful cutting can give you many options for using partial sadzas.

YOU'LL NEED:

* completed Sadza batik, 15 inches wide by 32 inches long
* lining fabric, 15 inches wide by 25 inches long
* fusible fleece, 14 inches wide by 31 inches long
* ⅝-inch diameter wooden dowels, cut into six 15-inch lengths
* 1½-inch screws
* wood glue
* paint for dowels (optional)

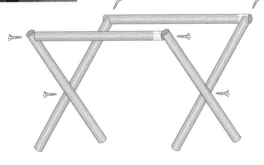

1 If desired, paint the dowels and let them dry completely. Arrange dowels as shown.

2 Drill small starter holes at the ends of the dowels, then assemble the X-shaped frame with cross pieces. Be careful not to over-tighten the screws; this might cause the dowel to split.

3 Fuse fleece to wrong side of sadza, centering fleece across fabric length and width. Turn under ½-inch on the long ends of both the sadza and the lining fabric. Press.

4 With right sides together, sew the short ends of the sadza and the lining fabric together.

Choose an interesting lining fabric, since it too will be visible.

5 Turn right-side out and press so that the ends of the sadza turn inward to form a facing. Machine-stitch along the seams where the fabric meets the lining fabric.

6 Hand-baste the long sides together, stitching close to the pressed edges, as shown above. Topstitch by machine.

7 Unscrew one side of each cross piece. Slip the sadza piece onto the dowel, and retighten the screw.

8 Working on a very level surface, shift the frame so it stands evenly. Reinforce all joints with a wood glue that dries clear.

9 As a decorative touch, make ties from remnants of the sadza and wrap these around the cross-joints as shown, applying more glue underneath the fabric ties.

CHAPTER 2
MARBLED FABRICS
(TURKEY)

MARBLED FABRICS are known for their intricate, plume-like designs, and no two marbled fabrics are the same. These designs might be most familiar to you as the inner lining papers used by book binders, evoking thoughts of stately libraries filled with fine, leather-bound volumes to last a lifetime.

You can create marbled fabrics in a limitless array of color combinations.

Marbling is a textile art that began as a way to decorate papers, emerging in various parts of the world at various times. The general procedure is characterized by the floating of pigments on liquid, the formation of designs in the pigments, and the transfer of the resulting designs onto the paper, fabric, or some other medium.

The technique we know as marbling is generally credited to tenth-century Turkish artisans. They called the process *ebru*, (or "cloud art"), and it was used to protect their most important personal and business documents from forgery! Because marbled objects are similar to snowflakes or even fingerprints in their individuality, they afforded a perfect safety measure; unscrupulous attempts to alter a marbled document once it was inscribed by a calligrapher were easily detected. As such, the craft became associated with secrecy and ritual, and even took on a mystical significance in Turk culture.

From Turkey, the technique was carried along trade routes to Persia, India, and later to countries in Europe. There is also evidence of one of the earliest marbled paper forms from Asia nearly 700 years ago. Japanese *suminagashi* (pronounced sue-me-nah-GAH-she) involves floating sumi inks on the water's surface, laying paper on top of the inks, then blowing on the water to create the swirling patterns. In this adaptation of marbling, there is little manipulation beyond the gentle fanning or blowing on the inks. The result is a more subtle look that appears as a natural phenomenon. The word literally means "ink-floating," and suminagashi had religious uses, among others. It was practiced by twelfth century Japanese Shinto priests, whose creations of black inks on white rice paper were used in divination ceremonies.

In Europe, marbling first appeared in the sixteenth century, when the papers were used as subtle, softly-colored backdrops for coats of arms and family trees. In addition, we find the technique employed again as a security measure; the edges of book pages were marbled, and any breaks in the patterns would indicate missing or stolen pages. Remember that at the time, books were not yet mass-produced, making them extremely valuable.

The following century would result in marbled box linings and book endpapers with deeper colors. Meanwhile, a Dutch interpretation of marbling is relatively more mathematical, where concentric circles were aligned in rows and columns.

Accessories for the home office or library are a fitting use for marbled fabrics in the home, given their bookbinding origins.

More recent marbling developments occurred in the 1960s, when bookbinding and decorative paper-making experienced a renaissance in Europe. A Spanish cottage industry sprung up, exporting beautifully marbled wrapping papers and greeting cards.

Today's resurgence in marbling brings us to designs on fabrics, most notably on cottons and silks. Marbled fabrics have gained new favor among wearable art enthusiasts, quilters, and home accessory designers.

Marjorie Lee Bevis is a professional marbler whose work is known to wearable artists and quilters internationally. In 1997, she traveled to Istanbul with other marblers from around the world, visiting sites where the Ebru masters worked. There, she studied the collections of artists past and present, including works by modern master Mustafa Duzgunman (1920-1990).

Bevis explains that Ebru designs were originally abstract, later developing into floral designs like the rose, tulip, carnation, poppy, and others. She also credits the introduction of acrylic paints in the 1950s for expanding the versatility of the craft beyond its book art origins, and through her company, Marbled Fabrics, she enjoys creating the cloth and educating people about the creative process in order to keep this unique craft alive.

DECORATING WITH MARBLED FABRICS

Marbling fits into many decorating schemes, simply because you control the colors and patterns. It can feature serene pastels with delicate swirls and floral shapes to grace a young lady's bedroom. Switch to standard feather motifs in darker tones of black, navy, plum, and brown, and marbled fabric easily finds a home in a rustic den with a masculine feel.

At first glance, the process seems complicated—even a bit intimidating—but it's fun and moves along quickly once you've experimented a bit with various paint manipulation techniques. This is the truly exciting and artistic part, where each cloth takes on its uniqueness.

Since marbling began in the bookmaking trade, apply your marbled fabric to these easy desk accessories that would be welcome in any library or other scholarly setting!

TRY MARBLING FABRIC!

You'll need to prepare both your fabric and the marbling solution well in advance of your marbling session. The supplies are available through mail-order (see Resource listings, page 108) and in art supply stores.

1 Prepare the fabric:

The *day before* you want to marble the fabric, prepare the fabric in an alum solution, to give the marbled designs permanency and washability. Wear rubber gloves—the alum chemical may irritate your skin.

a. Dissolve 3 tablespoons alum in 1 quart of cold water, stirring until the alum is completely dissolved.
b. Completely soak the fabric; once it is saturated, wring out the excess alum solution, smoothing out any wrinkles as much as possible, then let fabric air-dry.
c. To marble paper items, sponge alum onto the side to be marbled and allow it to dry.

2 Prepare the marbling solution:

a. *At least 12 hours ahead* of your marbling session, dissolve 3 tablespoons of carragheenan in 1 gallon of water in a blender. (Note: Since carragheenan is an organic thickening substance found in foods, it is safe to use in your regular kitchen blender.)

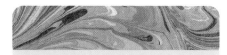

YOU'LL NEED:

* alum (a pretreatment for the fabric; makes designs permanent), also called aluminum sulfate
* fabric to be marbled (also paper, greeting cards, etc.)
* rubber gloves (for pretreating the fabric)
* carragheenan (thickens the water so paints will float on it)
* a wide tray for the carragheenan
* acrylic paints
* plastic or paper cups for paint mixing
* paint-mixing tools (flat wooden craft sticks or spoons)
* paint-dropping tools (eyedroppers, small whisk broom, flat wooden craft sticks, etc.)
* paint-designing tools (plastic combs, tooth picks, marbling rake, etc.)
* newspaper, cut into 2-inch-wide strips
* waterproof container (to discard wet newspaper strips)
* blender

Paints can be dropped in a uniform pattern, or randomly, as demonstrated by Karlton Herman, an innovative 11-year-old artist. Marbling is a great family activity!

Paints can be manipulated with combs, sticks, and other tools to create a variety of patterns.

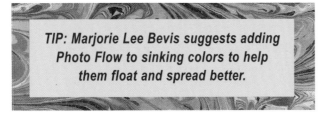

TIP: Marjorie Lee Bevis suggests adding Photo Flow to sinking colors to help them float and spread better.

b. Allow the mixture to stand undisturbed for at least 12 hours. This lets the mixture gel to the proper consistency and brings all air bubbles to the surface.

c. Pour solution into the tray. The solution should be 1 to 1½ inches deep in the tray.

3 Lay out the paints:

Paints should be of a consistency so that they drop easily, but are not too watery.

a. Squeeze or pour each color into a cup.

b. Blend any custom colors you like, and dilute paints with a bit of water, if needed. There are paints designed specifically for marbling; these are ready to use as they are.

4 Begin to marble:

a. With a strip of newspaper, skim off the top of the carragheenan immediately before you begin dropping the paints. This removes any last-minute dust or air bubbles from the surface.

b. Drop paints onto the surface, varying the colors, and continue until the paints "crowd" each other. Full coverage will ensure the best patterns. The paints should spread when dropped. If they sink to the bottom, they will not transfer to fabric.

c. Once you've floated all of the paints, use the combs, toothpicks, or other tools to manipulate it into various swirling patterns. Whatever you see on the surface is what will transfer to the cloth, so work until you are happy with the design. Unsatisfactory designs can be skimmed off with the newspaper strips, and you can begin again by floating new paint drops. The carragheenan will take on a muddy appearance, but this will not affect any new paints you add to the surface.

d. When you're happy with your patterning, hold fabric piece by the opposite corners and lower it onto the floating pattern, letting the center of the cloth touch down first, laying the remainder down in one smooth, fluid motion to avoid trapping any air bubbles. These will appear as white spots—skips or interruptions in the pattern.

e. Once the entire cloth has made contact with the solution, wait a moment, then lift it up using the same careful, continuous motion. The liquid that runs off the fabric is just excess carragheenan. The marble design is permanently set; however, since it is wet paint, handle with care and avoid having the marbled side of the fabric rub on itself. For paper projects, lay the piece onto the solution, pick it up, and lay it on a board or other flat surface; rinse gently and let dry.

f. If you are marbling more than one piece of fabric, store the first pieces in a plastic bag until you're done. Rinse fabrics in cold water, and then hang to air-dry thoroughly.

g. Machine-wash using a short, gentle cycle and mild soap.

h. To complete the process, dry the fabric and iron it to further heat-set the design.

5 To begin a new pattern, simply skim off the previous surface paint with the newspaper strips, then float fresh paints on the surface. The solution can be used repeatedly and can even be sealed tightly in a jar and stored for later use. Refrigeration allows the solution to be reused up to several weeks later.

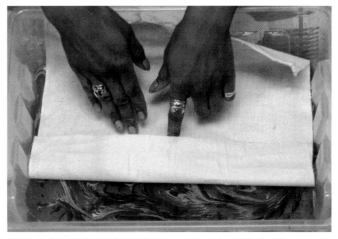

Smooth the fabric gently so it makes complete contact with the solution, to avoid blank spots in your design.

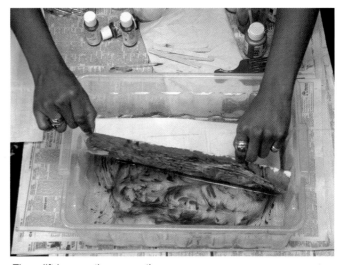

Then, lift in a continuous motion.

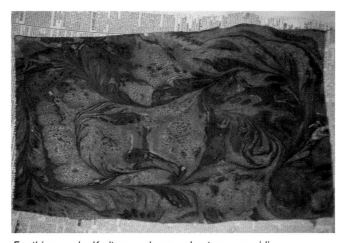

For this sample, Karlton used an egg beater as a swirling tool. Each tool, whether common or uncommon, offers its own special effects, so experiment and have fun!

The many colors in this fabric make it easy to pull out colors for trims, like the gold button, moss tassel, and moss faux suede base.

You'll Need:

- ☀ marbled fabric
- ☀ corrugated cardboard, 12 inches wide by 10 inches high
- ☀ ¾-yard paper-backed fusible web
- ☀ decorative trim (button, tassel, ornament, etc.)
- ☀ dense paperboard or thin wood for the stand
- ☀ remnant of coordinating fabric for the stand, at least 7 by 9 inches
- ☀ scissors
- ☀ iron
- ☀ glue gun and glue sticks

Marbled Fabric Desk Organizer

1 Cut cardboard into the shape shown at right and score down the center. Round the cardboard along the corrugated ribs to shape it. Flatten it out again.

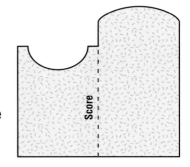

2 Apply fusible web to the wrong side of the marbled fabric and the fabric for the base, following the manufacturer's instructions.

3 Peel away the release paper and wrap fabric around the cardboard piece.

4 Fuse fabric to cardboard, snipping and turning in and fusing the raw edges as needed for a clean finish.

5 Again, fold at the score line and round out the two sides to form a pillow-box shape. Hot glue the open side of the box.

6 Cut base fabric into two pieces: one the size of the base plus at least ¾-inch all around, and a second, ½-inch smaller than the base.

7 Wrap the larger piece around the base and fuse, turning ends to the underside of the base. Cover these raw edges with the smaller piece and fuse.

8 Hot glue the bottom of the desk organizer to the base, positioning the organizer to be off-center for added interest.

Organizer

Base

Marbled Fabric Desk Trinket Box

1 For a padded lid, cut both fusible fleece pieces to the size and shape of the outer lid cardboard piece. Fuse one to the cardboard, and fuse the second to the first.

2 Apply fusible web to the wrong side of the marbled fabric, following the manufacturer's instructions.

3 Using the four round cardboard pieces as patterns, cut a circle of fabric for each, measuring 1 inch larger all around.

4 Peel the release paper from the fabric.

5 Cover the cardboard pieces (including the fleece-covered lid) with fabric pieces and fuse. To bring fabric neatly around to the underside of each cardboard piece, snip fabric to the cardboard, turn in the ends, and fuse as shown.

6 Placing these raw, uncovered sides together, glue inner lid to lid and inner base to base, carefully centering the inner pieces over the outer ones to assure a neat finish and a lid that fits properly.

7 Cover the strip of cardboard by cutting a strip of fabric large enough to completely cover both sides and overlap the width of the strip. Fuse.

8 Hot glue the strip just against the box base, applying a thin bead of glue where the strip meets the inner base. This forms the side of the box. Apply a small amount of glue where the ends of the strip meet.

9 Glue trim or embellishment to the lid, if desired.

The matching trinket box is perfect for paper clips, stamps, and other small desk essentials.

You'll Need:
- marbled fabric
- one 5-inch round box cardboard kit (see Home Arts in the Resources section.)
- paper-backed fusible web
- two 5-inch square pieces of fusible fleece (optional)
- iron
- scissors
- glue gun and glue sticks
- bead, trim, or ornament for the lid

CHAPTER 3

SASHIKO

(JAPAN)

This contemporary sashiko wall hanging offers a great sampling of popular stitch patterns.

Photo by Chuck Northup/Courtesy Eastwind Art

THIS SIMPLE yet beautiful quilting method had humble, purely utilitarian beginnings when it was used by rural Japanese women in the early eighteenth century. They would spend hours hand-stitching, to reinforce and add a measure of warmth to the work garments of their husbands, who were primarily fishermen, farmers, and lumberjacks.

Sashiko (pronounced SAH-shee-ko) is a plain, even running-stitch, normally a heavy white cotton or flax thread sewn through cotton fabric known as aizome cloth.

Asa cloths, a generic term for fabrics of hemp, flax, jute, or ramie, were also used for sashiko. These fabrics were dyed with indigo root to obtain a rich, dark blue hue.

Most of the stitched patterns were simplified images of things found in nature; clouds, ocean waves, blades of grass, bamboo, animals, and plants were just a few of the more popular motifs. There are also stitched representations of implements of war, characters from the written language, and tools. Later, larger, non-repeating designs with very specific meanings were adapted from family crests, or *Mon*.

The high-contrast look of clean white stitching on dark blue fabric showcases the

stitcher's skillful use of blank, or "negative," space as an integral part of the overall design. This quality is a distinctive element in all sashiko designs, and probably what I enjoyed best as I was preparing the practice pieces and the final samples for the placemats shown in this chapter.

Sashiko was originally used to reinforce and add warmth to clothing.

In Japan, every household had at least one person who could repair anything from clothing to dust cloths with sashiko, restoring threadbare items to a useful state. Sashiko mending sessions were a practical home art, as much as cooking, and served as part of a family's socialization time. In earlier days, many Japanese country homes featured a central sunken hearth that was the home's only source of light and heat. Here, families gathered to cook, eat, sew, and converse. In addition to a cooking fire, the hearth was used to heat a small hand iron for sewing. The hearth, and the household activities tied to it, became a symbol of hospitality.

Winter seasons were described as "two-layer" or "three layer" winters, for the amount of clothing one would wear to keep warm. It reflected the fact that the same garments were used year-round, made from crude, simple fabrics, and made warmer by the addition of sashiko stitching. It's no coincidence, then, that some of the best examples of sashiko are found in the colder northern regions of Japan's main island, specifically Tohoku. In addition to the amount of stitching needed to optimize warmth, the cold weather kept people inside—with plenty of time to perfect their needlecrafts and other home arts.

Jacket detail. Note the tiny, finely executed handstitches that make up the daisy motif. This pattern is a counted-stitch, worked on a grid for accuracy.

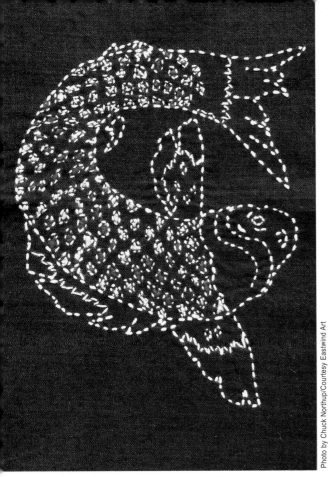

Photo by Chuck Northup/Courtesy Eastwind Art

Themes common in Japanese art, like this carp, are used often in modern sashiko. Note the newer introduction of red and pink threads along with the white.

Another important reason for sashiko's appeal was its ability to extend the life of a 100 percent cotton fabric, considered a precious and expensive commodity throughout the previous centuries. In fact, the owner of a pure cotton suit was considered prosperous.

By the 1700s, cotton became more accessible to the common people, and as its qualities of warmth and absorbency were discovered widely, attempts were made to begin cultivating cotton domestically.

Soon, cotton was plentiful, and the role of sashiko shifted from utilitarian to a more purely aesthetic role as the stitches became more decorative and elaborate. Refinement of one's sashiko skills had taken on such importance in Japanese culture that before marriage, a young woman often prepared ten work vests (enough to last a lifetime), covering them with sashiko for her future husband. As such, the ability to do sashiko well was an important characteristic of a good bride.

Another interesting indication of the significance of needlework in Japan is *Hari Kuyo*. This annual ceremony involves the gathering of all broken and bent needles in a household. These are taken to a Shinto shrine and stuck into blocks of tofu. It's believed that this ritual provided the now-defunct sewing tools a comfortable place to rest. During the ceremony, stitchers expressed gratitude for the tools that facilitated their work during the past year, and they prayed for the further mastery of sewing skills for the coming year. Thus, the necessary tools and fabrics for needlework in general, and sashiko in particular, hold a spiritual place within the culture.

DECORATING WITH SASHIKO

Sashiko gives any room a certain order and serenity. The clean, spare look of blue and white is great for kitchens, dining areas, even powder rooms and bedrooms.

Sashiko is an easily portable craft, especially in smaller projects like pillow fronts or stitched hand towels. (It lets you spend little pockets of time creatively, as I did recently while in the infamous line at the state motor vehicle agency to renew my driver's license.)

Considering the fact that I don't particularly enjoy hand stitching, I fell in love with sashiko and found it very relaxing. It's ironic that a stitch so simple requires such precise placement; a wayward stitch would easily disturb the "rhythm" of the piece overall.

One of the best guidelines I found was that each stitch should resemble a tiny grain of rice. This varies according to the number of layers stitched through (more layers require larger stitches), the weight of the thread, and the skill of the stitcher.

TRY SASHIKO QUILTING!

In addition to the patterns shown here, sashiko stencils are available for the most common designs (see Craft and Textile Supplies, page 109), as are all of the other necessary supplies. Authentic sashiko thread is a white or ivory unmercerized cotton that comes in soft bundles. It gives the softest, most desirable hand; however, alternatives include crochet thread or Perle cotton #5. You can also use multiple strands of standard embroidery floss.

1 Select desired patterns and transfer your design onto the fabric. Your stitches will be placed exactly along these lines, so it's important to mark the designs accurately.

2 If the back of your project will be concealed with a lining or backing fabric, simply knot the thread to begin. If the back side of stitching will be visible, secure the end of the thread by drawing the thread through the back, taking three smaller stitches; then go back, overlapping these stitches. Clip the thread end as close to the fabric as possible. Your thread should be securely anchored.

3 Begin stitching your design, running four to eight stitches per inch. Stitches should be evenly sized and spaced, as any variations will be noticeable in the end result. In general, straight lines are worked several inches (or up to fifteen to twenty stitches) at a time, to avoid curving of any of the stitches. Rounded lines are worked just a few stitches at a time for more precise stitch placement. If the fabric puckers, especially around curved stitching, hold the fabric taut as you stitch, gently stretching it back into its original shape.

4 End stitching by anchoring the thread in the same manner you began: draw thread to the back, run three or four small stitches, and go back, overlapping stitches over these. Cut thread close to the fabric.

YOU'LL NEED:

* indigo cotton or other dark blue, plain-weave fabric, prewashed and pressed
* sashiko thread
* white quilter's marking pencil or tailor's chalk
* hand-sewing needles (with a large eye, to accommodate the heavier thread)

Sample Sashiko Patterns

BASKETWEAVE

TORTOISE

WAVING GRASS IN THE WIND

OCEAN WAVES

WAVES (variation)

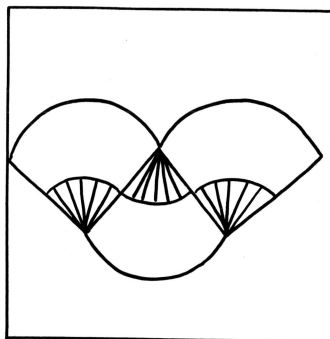

FANS

SASHIKO QUILTED PLACEMATS

Placemats trimmed with sashiko work are a perfect sampler for those new to the technique. Note that I've teamed it with an indigo cotton print, which is actually imported from Senegal! Take advantage of opportunities like this to mix fabrics from different cultures for a truly unique look. Unexpected combinations make for interesting conversation pieces.

Sashiko placemats add both style and serenity to casual dining.

TIP:
Notice that the sashiko inset is placed along one side of the placemat, not the entire top. Since the center of the placemat will be covered with a plate when in use, this asymmetrical design is a practical way to enjoy your handiwork throughout the meal!

YOU'LL NEED:

☀ sashiko supplies
   (listed on page 33)
☀ 1 yard contrast fabric
☀ thread
☀ sewing machine
☀ scissors

1 Transfer designs and work sashiko stitching on solid blue fabric as described above. Be sure to complete two sections, each measuring 12 inches long by 5 inches wide. In addition, cut two strips from the solid blue fabric, each measuring 2 inches wide by 12 inches long.

2 From contrast fabric, cut two pieces 19 by 13 inches for the backing. Cut one each for the top of the placemat: 2 inches wide by 13 inches long and 13 inches square.

3 Sew top pieces together as shown, using ½-inch seam allowances. Press seams open.

4 Pin top to backing, right sides together. Stitch, using a ½-inch seam allowance and leaving an opening for turning.

5 Trim corners; turn right-side out. Press.

6 Close the opening with small hand stitches.

Like most Japanese art, these fabric print designs feature naturalistic themes.

JAPANESE COTTON PRINTS

To complement the quiet, rhythmical look of sashiko, try mixing in Japanese cotton prints. These add a bit more color to the scene but will still work well in the same setting.

Familiar themes in Japanese prints are again nature-inspired, including carp (prosperity), butterflies (beauty), birds (happiness), and stylized representations of air and water. Nature appears as the primary inspiration in Japanese art in general because of its order, harmony, and evocative power, all qualities in which humankind exists and thrives. By surrounding oneself with these images, whether in textile form or other artistic media, one remains mindful of his or her connection to nature.

Try this decorative tabletop fan as an alternative to arrangements of flowers or fresh fruit.

JAPANESE PRINT ACCENT FAN

Folding fans of paper and bamboo were common to officials of the Imperial Court as early as the seventh century. Fans were often inscribed with love poems and exchanged in order to fan one's smoldering emotions.

The classic Japanese fan and its many variations are still viewed as objects of art, as well as practical personal accessories. Try this no-sew fabric version as a pretty alternative to floral arrangements on your dining table.

1 Cut fusible backing to the same size as the fabric.

2 Fuse backing to the wrong side of the fabric, following manufacturer's instructions. Let cool after fusing.

3 Fold fan in half lengthwise, wrong sides together, having long raw edges even. Steam-press firmly along the fold. Decide which side will be the front of the fan.

YOU'LL NEED:

(for a fan approximately 14 inches wide by 8 inches high)

* Japanese cotton print fabric, 1 yard by 16 inches wide
* 1 yard fusible craft backing
* paper-backed fusible web
* sturdy cardboard for base, at least 5 inches square
* coordinating decorative accents (brass, wood, dried flowers, etc.)
* glue gun and glue sticks
* craft knife
* scissors

4 Begin pleating at one end by turning under 1 inch and steam-pressing. Continue making 1-inch fan folds. As you create the folds, be sure that the folded edges line up evenly; this will affect the roundness of the finished fan, and any uneven raw edges at the bottom will be concealed later by the decorative accents. It's easiest to form the pleats by flipping the fan back and forth as you pleat, always keeping the new fold uppermost for optimum creasing. A shot of steam on each crease helps to set the pleats more quickly.

5 Once all pleats are set, hold them together loosely with rubber bands until completely cooled.

6 When cool, spread pleats out on a flat surface, arranging the fullness even-ly. Tack raw lower edges with a glue gun. If needed, trim off the last fold at each end so the last "rays" point toward the back of the fan.

7 For the base, cut two half-circles, about 4 inches in diameter. You can trace around the edge of a saucer or other round object for accurate shaping.

Permanent pleating is easy with a shot-of-steam iron. Work with the most recent pleat on top, directly under the iron.

8 Apply fusible web to a remnant of fan fabric or a contrasting fabric, then cut two half-circles, about 6 inches in diameter.

9 Remove the release paper, position each base piece in the center of the fabric, and fuse fabric to each base piece.

10 Glue one base to the fan front and one to the fan back, so that the fan's raw edges are just slightly above the bottoms of the half-circles.

11 Embellish the fan front with the decorative trims.

JAPANESE PRINT TABLE PAD

This very simple project can be sewn, or fusible web can be used for a no-sew version. It's an attractive and practical way to serve tea or other refreshments. It lets you protect one area of a pretty glass tabletop without completely concealing it with a full tablecloth.

1 Turn in 1 inch on all sides of the contrast fabric. Press.

2 Position fleece on the wrong side of the fabric as shown.

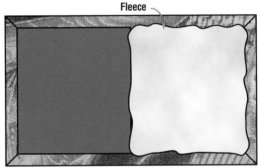

Fleece

Fabric

3 Fold fabric in half so that fleece is completely covered. Press.

4 Machine-sew, hand-sew, or seal the three open edges of the fabric with fusible tape.

5 Turn under 1 inch on all sides of the Japanese cotton print.

6 Position fabric in the center of the padded border fabric. Pin.

7 Machine-sew, hand-sew, or use fusible hem tape to attach the Japanese print to the contrast border.

8 Give the table pad a final press.

An easy table pad protects the table and beautifully accents an afternoon tea break. The metallic cotton border fabric brings out the subtle gold in the Japanese cotton print.

YOU'LL NEED:

* Japanese cotton print fabric, 10 inches square
* contrasting border fabric, 14 by 26 inches
* quilting fleece, 12 inches square
* fusible hem tape, or sewing machine thread
* scissors

CHAPTER 4

TAPA CLOTH
(SOUTH PACIFIC ISLANDS)

IMAGINE A FABRIC made without threads, weaving, knitting, or stitching of any kind, and you have a distinctive textile art known as tapa cloth, an ancient craft that continues today in the South Pacific.

Before the development of fabric looms, tapa cloths were created, serving both utilitarian and ceremonial functions.

Tapa is a Polynesian word for fabric that is made from the pulpy inner bark of indigenous trees, most often from mulberry trees. The entire bark is cut away from the tree, then soaked in sea water for about two weeks. From this, the soft inner bark is peeled away from the outer and cut into thin strips.

Next, the strips are pounded with a mallet, making them thinner, stronger, and more uniform. This process also results in a strip that is double its original width! Sometimes the strips are pounded together, edges overlapping, so the fibers mat and interlock; the fabric makers also join strips by sewing them, or by overlapping and gluing them together with a resin derived from the arrowroot plant.

Finally, this felted cloth, stronger and more durable than you might expect, is ready for the application of painted or stenciled designs. Stains made from various

As if the designs alone weren't dramatic enough, a common tapa length can be at least 7 feet long—perfect for doors or stairwells.

tree saps produce black, brown, and dark red stains. Other pigment sources are black or brown soot from burned candle nuts and red clay. The designs mimic items found in nature, such as foliage, birds, and sea life. More specifically, you'll see stylized starfish, banana leaves, seashells, and palm leaves. These are commonly combined with simple, repeating geometric motifs that work well as border designs. Many of the geometrics are patterns derived from Polynesian body tattooing. In some cases, the designs are applied so skillfully, and the cloth is covered so completely, that at first glance it's difficult to tell the painted areas from the backgrounds.

Pacific Islanders traditionally exchange gifts of textiles during special ceremonies, and it's believed that the positive "mana" of the woman who created a particular piece is inherent in the piece. This energy, or karma, also indicates the importance of the gift and bestows good fortune upon the receiver.

Tonga, a small island about four times the size of Washington, D.C., is known for its tapa, or *ngatu*, as these stunning textiles are more correctly termed. Located about one-third of the way from New Zealand to Hawaii, Tonga leads the Polynesian islands in production of the pounded and painted cloth. This is due to Tonga's geography and climate, which are perfectly suited to the cultivation of mulberry trees.

Throughout the Polynesian islands, the word "tapa" usually refers to the bark cloth before it is decorated, while ngatu is the finished, painted fabric. Earlier tapas were used in homes as room dividers and mat coverings, while ceremonial uses included floor coverings for special occasions, funerary gifts and offerings, and dance costumes.

Today, the fabric is still produced, and its usage is now almost exclusively limited to the ceremonial functions and special occasions related to the state and royalty.

The Maisin of Papua New Guinea have taken the craft's cultural significance a step further, as tapa-making has become the means by which they are able to preserve their rainforest. By turning to the production and sales of their indigenous textile art, the Maisin communities, who are strongly opposed to logging, have been able to fend off large financial offers from timber companies eager to purchase the rainforests. These efforts led to the development of Maisin Tapa Enterprises, a community-driven organization that purchases, promotes, and sells the textiles both nationally and worldwide. The resolve of this cooperative to sustain the region's most precious resources, while at the same time keeping the art alive, is inspiring.

A third South Pacific culture that is synonymous with creating fabric from tree barks is the people of Samoa, who refer to tapa cloth as *saipo*. Although Samoans do not use the terms interchangeably, they quickly learned what tourists were seeking when they asked for "tapa" cloths to purchase for souvenirs.

In Samoa, you'll find two methods for patterning the beaten cloth: *upeti* and *mamanu*. While mamanu designs are painted with natural dyes as described above, the upeti versions feature rub-off designs, formed by laying the plain saipo on a design tablet, usually leaves or carved wood. Dyes are then rubbed over the cloth, bringing out the carved motifs below. Upeti rubbed designs give a more subtle visual effect than the more common, higher-contrast painted bark cloths.

Textile artists in other parts of the world where the land is similarly well-wooded, not surprisingly, have their own interpretations of felted bark cloth. A comparable technique for nonwoven fabric production is found in central Africa among the Kuba and Pygmy groups, but the main difference lies in the type of trees used. Many of the beaten bark cloths from these parts of Africa are formed from fig tree bark, which oxidizes to a rich reddish-brown color over time, while the Pacific tapas made of mulberry bark remain off-white in color.

In the northeastern Republic of Congo, located in central Africa, the Mbuti fabricate a similar cloth as a communal activity; the men prepare the plain bark cloth, while women gather the pigments and paint the cloth. The making of bark cloth, like other aspects of Mbuti culture, is a pleasurable, social activity built on a spiritual foun-

Photo courtesy Malcolm Finaulahi Dreaneen

dation. Cloths are used in ritual dress and during weddings, funerals, and rites of passage.

A Caribbean version of bark cloth is still used among the Rastafarians, whose strict beliefs and lifestyle codes prohibit the use of any animal by-products, including clothing made of leather or other animal skins. The bark cloth is typically undecorated and is used for clothing as well as footwear.

Meanwhile, the Ainu in the northern region of Japan, also developed a tapa-style fabric, processing the fibers of atsui or elm trees, and using it primarily for clothing.

DECORATING WITH TAPA

What appeals to me most about this art form is the neutral, monotone designs. Shades of beige, black, and brown are always easy to incorporate into your existing scheme, whether a room features lots of wood furniture, metal pieces, or even glass accents. The hand-drawn geometrics and naturalistic themes give tapa a quality that is both ancient and contemporary at the same time. They also have a very unique texture that practically calls you over for closer inspection.

44 ✳ GLOBAL EXPRESSIONS

I'd probably hesitate to cut a tapa apart, preferring to hang an entire piece horizontally over a sofa, or vertically in a long, deep stairwell to maximize its dramatic impact. The shapes are often rectangular, with built-in bordering designs. When decorating with authentic tapa cloths, try working with the given size and shape to find the perfect spot for display. Purchased tapas can easily be 7 or 8 feet long by about 24 inches wide, sized right for door accents. In metropolitan Auckland, New Zealand, the larger mural-sized tapa cloths are used as a relatively inexpensive alternative to framed art, gracing the walls in studios and flats across the city.

Caring for tapa cloths is fairly easy. According to Malcolm Dreaneen, a Tongan tapa exporter based in New Zealand, it's best to simply keep the cloths dry and protected from sunlight. He points out that the cloth is very hardy and will likely outlast its owners! Another easy care tip: Should the layers begin to separate at the edges, repair them with the light use of a glue stick.

Adapt the dramatic look of tapa to a craft paper lampshade. The table covering is a contemporary, imported print that echoes tapa cloth as well as Polynesian cave paintings.

Try Tapa Designs!

The current popularity of paper-making lends itself to this natural extension, a paper lampshade decorated with tapa-inspired motifs. You can also purchase craft paper and distress it yourself for a weathered, antiquated look (as described in *African Accents: Fabrics and Crafts to Decorate Your Home*, Krause Publications, 1999, page 95).

TAPA CLOTH-INSPIRED LAMPSHADE

For the most authentic tapa influence, try shades of black, brown, and dark red paints on a cream or beige lampshade. Some tapas feature a single pigment color throughout the piece; others can contain more than one color.

YOU'LL NEED:
* paper lampshade
* acrylic paints
* containers for mixing paint colors
* paint brushes and flat wooden craft sticks

1 Lightly pencil in your choice of designs, combining them to create your own borders, etc. Begin at the back seam of the lampshade, so that if the spacing of repeats is not exact as you work around the shade and reach the starting point again, it will be less noticeable. A tapa's hand-drawn quality is important, so don't be overly concerned with perfectly straight lines.

2 Blend paint colors, if necessary. As a paint color dries on paper, the color can change slightly. I'd recommend making a small test blotch in an inconspicuous area, like the underside of the shade or the bottom edge, just at the seam. Allow it to dry and make any adjustments in the paint colors, if needed.

3 Fill in the designs with paint. Try using the rounded edge of a wooden stick to create straight, thick lines. It gives a more hand-drawn look than the paint brush, which I used more for filling in the solid areas.

4 Allow to dry thoroughly.

Sample Tapa Cloth Patterns

CHAPTER 5

TRAPUNTO
(ITALY)

TRAPUNTO IS a three-dimensional quilting technique that is widely believed to have originated in Italy in the 1500s, although some estimates place its origins in the 1300s. Known as a wholecloth quilting style, trapunto is worked on a single, or whole, piece of fabric, as opposed to a quilt top that is made up of many small fabric pieces stitched together.

Trapunto in its earliest form involves a top layer of fabric and a backing fabric stitched together by hand to form the outlines of various designs. The back layer would be carefully slit open, allowing for small amounts of batting to be inserted to create the raised design. The slit would then be sewn up with nearly invisible stitches; sometimes a third layer of fabric was added to the back to conceal less-than-perfect handwork. To add further definition to the raised areas, the quilter would add all-over stitching throughout the background. This flattens the background, increasing the contrast between raised and non-raised areas. The use of brown thread on ivory or light beige fabrics also increased the textural effect.

Trapunto enjoys a history as the fabric of Italy's aristocracy. Create this regal trapunto headboard for yourself (or a guest bedroom) for a bit of luxury.

This textile art developed as a purely decorative touch, trimming the garments and furnishings of wealthy Mediterraneans. Most popular were intricate designs featuring leaves, grapes, and vines, inspired by Sicilian vineyards and landscapes. Larger trapunto pieces, such as bed coverlets or wall hangings, might show entire scenes with raised figures like Medieval knights, princes, elegant ladies, and even phrases lettered in Sicilian dialect.

No doubt trapunto was a luxury to be enjoyed only by the wealthy, due to the painstaking handwork and the expensive fabrics; fine linens, wools, Persian silks, taffeta, and satins were preferred among the aristocracy. Solid white and ivory fabrics were considered the best for showing off even the smallest details. However, Trapunto can also be used to accent particular parts of a preprinted fabric, such as leaves or geometric designs.

One reason trapunto was used as an accent (such as on a garment cuff or small pillow) was the fact that it was rather time-consuming. As machine techniques came along, the options were broadened, enabling stitchers to complete larger projects quicker and more easily.

Various styles of trapunto developed in Europe, though the craft still remained fairly centralized in Italy and Europe's southern region. One style, known as *Florentine trapunto*, featured a sheer organdy top fabric, paired with an opaque bottom fabric of simple muslin or percale. The semitransparency of the top layer gave the trapunto a softer, more delicate look. In this case, the design was drawn on the back layer.

Other creative advances, such as colored and metallic threads, became popular for the quilt borders, and various touches of embroidery further enhanced the raised designs. In some cases, custom beadwork was added, resulting in the most stunning examples of trapunto work. Other designs revealed a military influence, adapting the look of quilted padding found on suits of armor.

Corded quilting was a new variation on trapunto that also became popular by the 1600s. As the name implies, two closely spaced, parallel rows of stitching are stuffed with a continuous length of cotton piping cord, for a thin, uniform design. This cording technique was quite effective for depicting vines, stems, and other thin elements in trapunto designs. Naturally, these newer design innovations became an escalating measure of wealth among the aristocracy.

DECORATING WITH TRAPUNTO

Unadorned or fully embellished, trapunto quilting interest has grown as new and easier methods have developed, including machine-sewn trapunto. Today's styles are popular for wall hangings, bed coverlets, pillows, and window valances. The luxurious effect and rich, noble history of trapunto make it a perfect bedroom accent, especially in luxe silk douppioni or satin—fabrics with sheen that really play up the "light and shadow" characteristics of trapunto detailing.

Another interesting home décor application for trapunto is the nursery. The padded effect makes it both pretty and practical for crib bumpers and other comforting room accessories. Make these in an easy-care cotton sateen instead of silk douppioni as mentioned above. Another benefit of using trapunto techniques in baby room décor is that the fabric itself creates beautiful, tactile designs; there's no need to embellish it with buttons, beads, or other infant-related safety hazards.

Trapunto is a great way to showcase culture-specific motifs. Imagine Chinese letter characters, intricate Celtic knots, or the maze-like designs found in Kuba raffia fabrics from the Congo region in central Africa, all expressed in this unique three-dimensional form. Any of these would be striking alternatives to the more traditional Italian Renaissance-inspired looks that trapunto usually incorporates. Consider these exciting possibilities for the Trapunto Headboard project below.

TRY TRAPUNTO QUILTING!

This is a quicker, simplified version of trapunto, as compared to the individual slashing and stuffing for each shape. In planning your project, such as a pillow, remember to allow a few extra inches to your fabric measurement, since the design stitching will cause the fabric to "draw up" a bit. This slight shrinkage amount will vary according to the amount of stitching in the piece.

Test-stitch, using both a regular sewing machine presser foot and the free-motion feature, to see which suits you best as you maneuver around the shapes. For the greatest control, trapunto can also be hand-stitched.

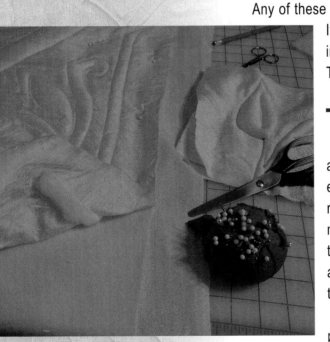

Note the leaf design in the test sample, which can then be made into a pillow.

TRAPUNTO HEADBOARD

Give your bedroom a regal look with this soft-sculptured alternative to a wooden or metal headboard. Simple hanging tabs give you the opportunity to show off a beautiful drapery rod at the same time. You can even match the rod to your bed frame type for a custom decorator look, whether it's brass, wrought iron, or wood.

1 Measure the width of the bed. Both the fabric and backing should measure this width, plus 8 to 10 inches. The length should measure 40 inches. If needed, you can piece the fabric at both ends, working these vertical seams into your design, as shown in the photo.

2 Enlarge the designs given, or create your own. Transfer or trace the designs onto the top fabric, leaving at least a 3-inch border all around that is free of design lines to allow for finishing of the edges. If using an air-soluble pen, refer to the pen manufacturer's instructions and be sure to test it on your fabric to be sure the markings disappear.

3 Pin 1-inch-thick batting to the wrong side of the marked <u>test</u> fabric.

YOU'LL NEED:
- top fabric: silk douppioni, satin, cotton sateen (see notes in step 1 regarding yardage)
- dense quilt batting, 1-inch thick
- low-loft quilting fleece or fusible fleece
- backing fabric
- decorative drapery rod and finials
- safety pins
- thread
- sharp scissors
- sewing machine
- air-soluble marking pen

TIP: Make small practice pieces of trapunto to get the feel of the technique, then use these smaller pieces to make coordinating throw pillows for the bed.

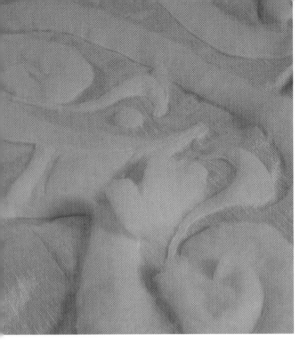

High-loft batting makes trapunto easy, compared to the original slashing and stuffing of each individual motif. Simply trim away the excess batting after stitching it to the top layer, following the design lines.

4 Pin 1-inch-thick batting to the wrong side of the marked project fabric. Secure with safety pins or baste into place with large running-stitches throughout the piece.

5 Using your test piece first, machine- or hand-stitch along the lines of the design, through both thicknesses. Hold layers taut in all directions as you stitch. Depending on the intricacy of your chosen design, you might prefer to use your sewing machine's free-motion setting to sew along the lines, with the feed dogs lowered. After some practice stitching, continue with the headboard piece.

6 Once all stitching is completed, turn piece over. Cut away batting from areas you do not want raised, so that batting remains under the design areas (swirls, flower petals, etc.), as shown in the photo, right. Cut the batting close to the stitching, *very carefully*, to avoid cutting the top fabric layer.

7 Layer the low-loft fleece (or fusible fleece, with fusible side up) over the wrong side of the backing fabric. Then, layer the trapunto top, right-side up. Pin all layers together with safety pins, distributing fullness evenly.

8 Begin stitching either at the center of your design, or with the largest motifs. As an alternative to the free-motion stitching, using a zipper foot will allow you to stitch close to the raised areas. Keep the fabric taut as you sew to prevent puckering, especially as you complete the stitching at the end of a motif. Stitch over the previous outline stitching as much as possible. If regular low-loft fleece is used, random stipple quilting through the background will flatten it against the raised designs. If fusible fleece is used, carefully touch iron down on the background areas so that the fleece adheres to the top fabric. Be sure to cover your fabric with a press cloth to avoid any scorch marks or leftover fusible resins from your iron surface.

9 Trim away 1½ inches of low-loft fleece around all sides of the headboard.

10 Turn 1½ inches of the backing fabric in over the fleece and press.

TIP:
As with any quilt project, note that the more stitching there is, the more the size will "draw up." For a design with lots of detail, consider adding an extra allowance to all sides so that the finished piece will still span the width of the bed easily.

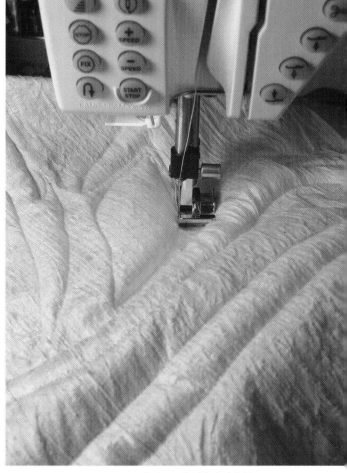

11 Turn under 1 inch of the top fabric and press.

12 Prepare four hanging tabs for a twin bed, five for full or queen, and six tabs for a king-size bed.

a. For each tab, cut one square of fabric and one of low-loft or fusible fleece, each measuring 7 inches square.

b. Position fleece against the wrong side of the fabric; fuse fleece to wrong side of fabric, if applicable.

c. Turn under ½-inch on two opposite sides of each tab, catching in both the fabric and the fleece. Hand-stitch or hem with fusible tape.

d. Fold tab, wrong sides together and baste raw edges together.

e. Pin one tab at each end of the headboard, between the top and backing fabrics, 2 inches in from each side edge.

f. Pin remaining tabs, spacing them evenly across the top.

g. Line up the top, sides and bottom of the headboard front and back so that the front slightly overlaps the back. Pin.

h. Machine-stitch layers together, reinforcing the stitching along the tabs at the top edge of the headboard.

13 Slip headboard tabs onto the rod on the wall, and install drapery rod at the desired height, according to rod manufacturer's instructions.

A zipper foot is helpful in sewing around the shapes. Free-motion stitching is also used. Try both and use the method you're most comfortable with.

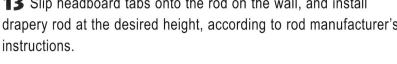

TIP: To accentuate the designs further, try thread in a contrast color, or a heavier thread such as buttonhole twist or upholstery thread. Using clear monofilament thread will allow only the raised areas themselves to be visible.

SAMPLE TRAPUNTO PATTERNS

TRY CORDED QUILTING!

This variation of trapunto features parallel channels of stitching, each filled with yarn (for a softer feel) or cording (for a firmer hand). Corded quilting is a great visual accent for bordering pillows, duvet covers, wall hangings, even placemats or clothing. Corded quilting can be worked in simple lines, or can create specific motifs, and is often used along with basic trapunto work in the same project. As with trapunto, the effect is best seen when worked on solid color fabrics.

It's important to experiment with the amount of filling yarn or cording you'll need; too little will fail to create the proper effect, while overstuffing can cause puckers and stiffness in the finished piece.

YOU'LL NEED:
- top fabric
- backing fabric
- filler: yarn or cotton piping cord (If possible, match the color of the filler to the top fabric.)
- sewing machine
- thread
- blunt tapestry needle

1 If needed, draw your design on the back fabric. Machine-stitch along the lines to create channels.

2 Thread tapestry needle with filler. A double or triple strand of yarn might be necessary. Cotton cording used for piping comes in various widths so that only one strand should suffice, depending on the size of your channels. Working from the back fabric, test-run through two or three adjacent channels to determine the right amount of filler needed. Make adjustments in the number of strands as needed.

3 As you draw the needle from the back to fill spaces between the stitches, bring the needle back out as you approach curves or corners. Work the needle back through the same hole to continue filling. Leave a bit of slack in the stitches as you work to prevent puckering.

4 At the end of the design, bring needle through to the back. Push the filling ends under the backing fabric.

5 Press the completed fabric face down on a padded pressing surface, or an ironing board covered with a folded towel; press lightly.

CHAPTER 6

BLOCK PRINTING
(INDIA)

INDIAN TEXTILES are my own second-favorite as a category, from embroidered saris to tapestries. One of my most exciting discoveries in this area of world textiles is block-printed fabric.

The "block" refers to a solid piece of wood, into which lacey, intricate patterns are carved. A cloth pad is placed in a container, then inks or dyes are added, saturating the pad. The block is pressed into the pad to pick up the color, and stamped repeatedly onto a sheet of cloth to create a continuous design.

Fabrics can be monotone, or may feature as many as eight to ten different colors, resulting in sophisticated, richly detailed arrangements. Multiple borders and sometimes a large central design are characteristic of traditional block-printed fabric, which is usually a lightweight cotton.

The artist's skill lies not only in his ability to combine the colors and patterns well, but also in the registration of the design.

This quilted coverlet shows good registration in the all-over design. Bed coverings are a popular application of bordered block print designs, both in India and around the world.

Registration refers to how accurately each stamped image is lined up to the next, producing a cloth with well-matched repeats for a flawless, uninterrupted look. Accurate alignment is ensured by the use of registration notches cut into the blocks, or by brass pins inserted into the corners of the blocks. These are matched to the previous markings with each imprinting of the cloth.

Around the world, fabrics have been produced in a similar stamping fashion, including ancient Chinese letterpress printing and adinkra stamping in Ghana, which are highly symbolic designs carved into gourds instead of wood blocks.

India's block prints have led the way because of the innovative dyeing methods and the precise carvings found in centers such as Gujarat, India. In fact, the wonderfully ornamental designs of expert Gujarati carvers can still be found to grace the entrances of royal palaces. The high degree of detail in the carving is achieved by the use of hard, densely grained woods such as ash, sycamore, or pear wood. These woods are so dense that the weight of the stamp became a consideration, and in some cases, a larger design had to be divided into several stamps for easier and more accurate handling by the fabric artist.

The price of each cloth increases with the quality of printing and design complexity, although the fabrics are still produced relatively inexpensively. Such affordability makes the fabrics both popular and accessible worldwide.

Block-printed fabrics are fun and easy to make, and colors and designs can be made to fit any décor or color scheme. Easy-to-carve rubber and synthetic blocks offer a simple alternative to carving wood blocks because of their uniform shapes and softer, more cuttable surfaces. You might be able to locate authentic wood blocks through dealers; however, they are not easily found, and if you are successful in finding the real ones, these might be best saved for a collectible display and design inspiration for carving your own non-wood blocks, rather than actual use.

Looking for a great source of Indian block printing designs? Try the patterns and motifs used in mendhi body painting. This ancient personal embellishment is a kind of temporary tattoo made with dyes from the henna plant. It is an art form that dates back for centuries mostly in India, northern Africa, and the Middle East. The scrolls, florals, leaves, medallions, and other lacey, open patterns used in mendhi are comparable to the wood block carvings.

The handstitching throughout somewhat resembles sashiko, simply following the outlines of the block printing.

DECORATING WITH BLOCK PRINTS

Many designs are sized for bedding and sold as twin, full, queen, or king sizes, often featuring central medallion motifs and multiple borders. They make beautiful quilt tops or duvet covers, backed with a coordinating solid or printed fabric and embellished with even the simplest hand stitching. Because of their size, dramatic layouts, and light weight, they also make great bed canopies or window treatments (lined), and can even be used to "upholster" a wall or drape a table, bookcase, or mantle. Backed with a clear plastic liner, you can even create a shower curtain, making use of the borders along the top and/or bottom of the shower curtain.

To make a lightweight block-printed fabric more versatile as a blanket, it is often backed with a second fabric, either plain or in a less elaborate coordinating block print design. These are placed wrong sides together, then hand-stitched throughout with a plain running-stitch that resembles a sashiko stitch. The difference is that while sashiko stitches themselves create the patterns, hand-stitched Indian block-printed blankets are stitched along the printed designs. The edges of the blanket are turned inside about ¾-inch and bound with a simple running-stitch.

TRY BLOCK PRINTING!

There are several choices of materials for making your own blocks. Linoleum is popular because its durability provides a consistent image, but because it's rigid, it's more difficult to carve into than the flexible, rubbery types. All are fairly easy to find through art materials retailers and mail order sources (see Craft and Textile Supplies, page 110).

YOU'LL NEED:

* linoleum block or rubber carving block
* cutting tools for block printing
* acrylic paints
* textile medium for paints (optional)
* plain weave fabric for printing

1 Lightly pencil in your design on the surface of the block, remembering that the stamped image will be the reverse of what you draw because the stamp will be inverted when you print. Keep this in mind, especially if your stamp design contains letters or one-way designs. Make a few practice cuts in a corner of the block with the different blades to get familiar with their cutting effects. Follow guidelines on the cutting tools package for further instructions.

2 Cut your block design. Cut a small notch in one side of the block to act as the registration mark. This will help you to line up the stamp after each impression, so the motifs appear as a single, continuous design.

The right supplies make it easy to create your own stamps. My design was cut freehand; you can draw your own, or trace one of the designs given on pages 64 and 65.

The linoleum block (upper left) and flexible stamp materials are practical choices for block printing projects. The flexible stamp (carved) is similar to a large slab pencil eraser, but even smoother on the surface.

3 Blend paint colors, if needed, and apply paints to the block with a paintbrush. (Adding textile medium will give the fabric an added degree of washability because it helps the paints to become more permanently embedded into the fabric. Depending on your intended end use of the fabric, textile medium may or may not be needed. Follow manufacturer's instructions for usage.) Try varying the colors on a single stamp to replicate the multicolored designs in Indian block printing.

4 Do some test prints on scrap fabric. If possible, use fabric scraps that are large enough to "become something" if the images come out perfectly the first time. A small pillow or a block for use in a quilt or placemat are just a few ways to use your test pieces.

Try printing colors in layers for an interesting effect, or ink the stamp with several colors at one time. Note the authentic wood block at the top left, used for the window shade project.

Make any necessary adjustments to the stamp, such as cutting deeper into the block, or making narrow cuts slightly wider for more definition. Place fabric on a flat surface. It might help to tape down the edges to keep it taut while printing.

5 Press the block down into the fabric, then lift the block carefully to avoid smudges.

6 Using the registration notch, plan the positioning of the next image, ink the stamp again, if needed, and press down. Repeat until the entire cloth is filled to your satisfaction.

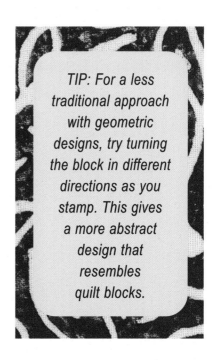

TIP: For a less traditional approach with geometric designs, try turning the block in different directions as you stamp. This gives a more abstract design that resembles quilt blocks.

Border treatments like this are a common usage of block printing.

INDIAN BLOCK-PRINTED WINDOW SHADE

This project highlights the use of block printing as solely a border application. Most block printing is done on relatively smooth fabric, but I chose a burlap to see the effect of the printed images on a highly textured fabric. The burlap gave a less sharp image for an interesting faded or "weathered" look. Be creative and experiment with different fabrics to discover new looks.

1 Follow kit instructions to measure, cut, fuse, and complete the no-sew window shade.

2 Plan the design:

a. Measure the block size, and figure out the number of full repeats you'll be able to fit across the lower portion of the shade.

b. Mark the center of the shade lightly in pencil; this is the placement mark for the center of the first stamped image.

c. Continue on either side of the first image, using your registration marks to line up the block accurately each time you print. If your registration is still a little "off," or some of the images don't show up completely, you can carefully fill in these gaps with a bit of paint on a paint brush or flat wooden craft stick.

3 At either end, you can choose to stamp a partial image, having the design run directly off the fabric edge, or end on a full repeat, leaving a bit of blank space at each end of the design. With a medallion-style block, place designs at the center of the shade, both above and below the border design.

4 Let dry completely, and install roller shade according to kit instructions.

YOU'LL NEED:

* burlap, or the fabric of your choice
* Fuse-A-Shade™ fabric roller
* shade kit
* carved printing blocks
* acrylic paints
* fine paint brush or flat wooden craft stick

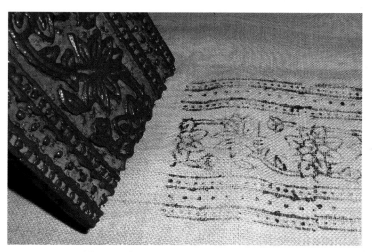

You may find it helpful to test your block print before placing the design on the project fabric.

Touching up the pattern is simple.

SAMPLE BLOCK PRINTING PATTERNS

INDIAN EMBROIDERIES

Another Indian textile specialty with lots of home décor potential is embroidery. Embroideries clearly reflect the cultural concept that one's ability to make beautiful things brings about good fortune and plays an important social role in various phases of his or her life. These creations are densely covered with cotton and metallic threads, beadwork, cording, fabric remnants, and small *shisha* mirrors.

The finest embroidered fabrics are reserved for marriages, religious ceremonies, and festivals, while others are used to furnish homes and even to outfit horses, camels, and mules. It's customary for Indian girls to begin stitching their dowries as young as age six, and through the years, embroidery plays a vital part in family life, as needlework pieces continue to be handed down through generations. Embroidery needles dating back to 2000 B.C. have even been uncovered in a number of archeological digs and land excavations over time.

Silk, cotton, and wool threads that were originally colored with natural dyes have been mostly replaced with synthetically dyed yarns. However, basic stitches remain the most popular, including satin, herringbone, chain, running, and couching stitches, variations that are found around the world. Generally, smaller sections of embroidery are stitched and embellished. Then, these sections are joined together and backed with a common fabric to create a large piece.

Inspiration from the variety of stitches and textures contained in a piece gives you a great opportunity to experiment with the many stitch patterns and other applications available on computerized sewing machines. Combine these with hand techniques for a more authentic look. Joining fabrics of different weights is easy if you first reinforce lighter weight fabrics with fusible interfacing. This gives you a more substantial fabric that is better able to hold up to the many embellishments and stitch designs you might want to add.

Remember to vary the shades and colors so that the details stand out, even if you're working within one color family, like the red, rust, and brown tones shown here.

INDIAN EMBROIDERY FOOTREST

Lifestyle note: Although this fabric is relatively heavyweight, the fine handwork in it suggests a certain fragility, especially if the piece is older. Consider this project as a decorative accent to be placed and enjoyed in a "low traffic" area, such as your bedroom or a quiet meditation space.

One option to increase the practicality of an embroidered footrest would be to use the decorative fabric along the sides of the footrest, topping it with a more durable coordinate, such as upholstery fabric or an industrial-weight faux suede. Leather is another interesting choice for the top of the footrest.

Measurements are given for the footrest shown; you can alter the length, width, and height as desired.

Protect the delicate nature of fine Indian embroideries by placing them in low-traffic areas, like this meditation area.

YOU'LL NEED:

(for a footrest 14 inches long, 10 inches wide, and 8 inches high)
- heavy embroidered fabric, large enough to cover the entire footrest frame
- coordinating top fabric (optional), at least 22 inches square
- plywood, ⅜-inch thick: two side pieces, each 6 by 12 inches
  two side pieces, each 6 by 10 inches
  one top piece, 13 by 11 inches
- particle board, ⅛-inch thick: one bottom piece, 13 by 11 inches

(both the plywood and the particle board can be purchased <u>and</u> cut to size at Home Depot or your local lumber shop)

- fabric to cover particle board bottom (optional)
- 2-inch-thick foam rubber, 14 by 12 inches
- ¾-inch-thick, foam rubber (to cover each of the side pieces)
- glue gun and glue sticks
- hammer and small finishing nails
- staple gun and staples (heavy duty)
- four thumbtack-style "chair feet," about 1-inch diameter, or four large wooden ball feet

I love the depth and variety of embellishments in this piece, from shisha mirrors and metallic threads to the use of couching, patchwork, and embroidery throughout

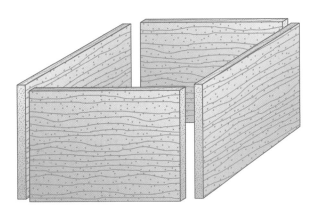

1 Form the sides of the footrest by nailing pieces together, as shown at left.

2 Glue ½-inch thick foam rubber pieces to each side. Center the top of the footrest over this piece, centering it over the four corners.

3 Nail top board in place.

4 Glue 2-inch-thick foam rubber to the top, centering it over the four corners.

5 Cover footrest with the embroidery piece.

a. Starting on one of the short sides, staple fabric to the lower edge of the plywood, placing staples into the ⅜-inch thickness of the wood.

b. Pull fabric across the top of the footrest firmly but not too tightly.

c. Staple the opposite short side in the same manner.

d. Tuck in the corners, creating fold that lines up evenly with the sides of the footrest.

e. Pull fabric down over long sides of the footrest and staple along the edge of the plywood as before.

6 If you are using a coordinating fabric for the top:

a. Wrap it over the top and staple one fabric edge to one side of the footrest.

b. Pull taut from the opposite side of the footrest; staple the remaining sides, pulling taut, and overlapping corners for a neat finish.

c. From the embroidery fabric, create a length that measures 46 inches long by 8½ inches high. Turn under 1 inch at the top of this piece. Staple to the upper edge of the footrest, close to the fold of the fabric, neatly encasing all raw edges of the coordinating top fabric.

d. Staple fabric to lower edge of footrest.

e. Starting on one of the short sides, staple fabric to the lower edge of the plywood, placing staples into the ⅜-inch thickness of the wood.

f. Staple the opposite side, and continue with remaining sides.

7 Cover particle board with fabric, wrapping raw edges of the fabric around to the back. Glue.

8 Turn footstool wrong-side up; position the bottom piece over the four sides, keeping all edges of the decorative fabric inside.

9 Use small nails to secure bottom board to the footrest.

10 If needed, paint nail heads and staples with an acrylic paint color that blends in with the fabric.

CHAPTER 7
MOLA APPLIQUÉ
(PANAMA)

THE SAN BLAS ISLAND region, located just off the Caribbean coast of Panama, is home to the Kuna (or Cuna) Indians, and is well known for a textile tradition called mola, a form of reverse appliqué.

Mola art, mastered by Kuna women, is an intricate cutwork technique created with several layers of fabric. These are usually bright solid colors. An upper layer design is cut out, and its raw edges are tucked in and neatly hand-stitched to expose the under layers. Additional upper layers can also be added and cut, exposing previous layers through their own cutouts. The panel is sometimes decorated with standard appliqué and embellished with embroidery stitching.

Experts are able to cut and work their designs as they go, without drawing them first.

Traditional molas primarily feature deep red and black, with a wide variety of bright colors in between. Abstract and highly stylized animals, reptiles, birds, and sea creatures, found in the natural surroundings of the San Blas coastlines and rain forests, are common subjects stitched into these multilayered textiles. Others are scenes depicting people and everyday objects, marriage, death, rites of passage, legends, or historical references.

Mola reverse appliqués are not for the shy-of-color! Use them to brighten up a neutral area.

Sometimes, seemingly unrelated motifs are combined in the same mola panel, a design characteristic popular with current mola artists. For example, a mola showing a chicken holding a broom, or a tiger carrying a basket containing a small puppy, would not be considered at all unusual!

These themes represent a relatively modern style of mola design; many years ago, molas featured simpler, geometric designs, an important clue for collectors in attempting to date a mola piece. Other indicators of an older mola are the use of cotton that is slightly coarser than later pieces, and the appearance of printed fabrics among the under layers, as compared to the exclusive use of solids in newer molas.

Red and black are the traditional base colors of mola design. This contemporary framed piece is styled after earlier molas, which were geometrics as opposed to the stylized objects found in modern pieces.

Sizes vary, but they average around 13 by 18 inches, or roughly the size of a placemat.

Culturally, mola-making plays an important part in a girl's development. Her skills are expected to increase as she gets older, resulting in the completion of approximately one dozen quality molas before she reaches marriage age in her late-teens or early twenties. The designs might be whimsical themes like those mentioned before, but the handwork itself is regarded as serious business.

The finest of these hand-stitched panels form the front and back bodices of blouses worn by the women. Mola images for one's personal wardrobe are chosen with care and are viewed as a direct reflection of the stitcher/wearer. The yoke and sleeves of the blouse can be made of commercially printed or solid fabric. Completing the conventional Kuna woman's outfit are a knee-length wrap skirt, a bright red and yellow head wrap, beaded arm and leg bands, and a gold nose ring.

Molas hold great economic significance for the Kuna, too. Less elaborate versions created for the tourist trade are marked by fewer fabric layers, less embroidery, and larger slashes. There are two reasons for the difference in quality between personal molas and those produced for souvenirs and export. First, tourists are generally not as familiar with the intricacies of the finer pieces, so there is less appreciation for them (at least among non-fabricholics!). Second, the tourists' aesthetic preferences tend to lean more toward the simpler, less detailed pieces.

Nevertheless, outside interest in molas is considerable, allowing many of the mola artists to supplement their incomes significantly. A cooperative was organized to encourage heightened skills in mola-making, and to develop the markets further. Sales and merchandising efforts through the co-op outlet store in Panama City, along with export sales to the United States, are run entirely by the Kuna women. This special art form provides them with more than a creative outlet; it also affords them a high degree of economic independence and social status.

Display a piece of art as you conceal the clutter of a bar, bookcase, or other open storage area.

DECORATING WITH MOLA APPLIQUÉ

Bringing mola designs into your home is fun and easy, because they're so vibrant and eye-catching. Their size is perfect to brighten up a hallway or small wall area. They can't easily be cut because of the many layers and extensive amounts of hand-stitching, so consider creative decorating ideas that use the molas as complete panels.

☀ Add small hanging tabs in coordinating fabric to the upper edges of the mola. Hang it from the back of a dining chair or accent chair.

☀ Make accent pillows (for basic pillow directions, see Chapter 8 – Indonesian Batik, page 87).

☀ Create a larger wall hanging using the mola as a central block. Piece other fabrics around it, choosing either solids, texture prints, or multicolored cotton prints, incorporating the predominant colors in the mola.

☀ Hang it on a wall, framed or unframed.

☀ Cover the front of a small bookcase or a nightstand. Attach the mola to the upper edge with a pushpin in each corner. If the mola is too narrow to span the width of the bookcase or table, add coordinating fabric pieces as for the wall hanging above. This great "double duty" use lets you display a work of art, while concealing an untidy shelf or small storage area. I use Kuba raffia fabric squares from Central Africa in a similar fashion.

☀ Try the magazine holder shown in sadza batik in Chapter 1, page 18.

☀ Sandwich the mola between a Plexiglas top and particleboard bottom for a unique desk blotter or table accent. Carefully glue just the four corners with an all-purpose craft cement that dries clear.

Note: Authentic molas may not be finished along the edges. There are two easy ways to finish the edges:
☀ Option 1:
1. Simply cut a piece of coordinating fabric the size of the mola.
2. With right sides together, sew along the sides, using a seam allowance small enough to avoid sewing through the design.
3. Leave an opening for turning.
4. Turn and press.
5. Close the opening using small, neat hand stitches.
☀ Option 2:
1. Encase the raw edges in a double-fold seam binding.
2. Sew close to the fold of the binding around all sides by machine or hand. (This works as long as the back fabric of the mola is in good condition.)

TRY MOLA APPLIQUÉ!

For the most authentic look, be sure to include deep red and black, along with a good variety of brights. No special stitching experience is needed, but it might be helpful to try cutting, turning, and neatly stitching a few practice layers before you begin.

The motifs on page 78 can be used singly for small projects, enlarged, or combined for a larger piece with geometric designs used in between.

YOU'LL NEED:

* assorted solid color fabrics
* hand-sewing needles
* thread (match to color of the top layer)
* sharp, small embroidery scissors
* embroidery floss (optional)
* Liqui-Fuse™ fusible glue (optional)

Molas are carefully built layer by layer, color by color.

1 Stack fabrics in the desired color order. Using three to five fabrics is a good start for a first project.

2 Baste fabrics together around the edges. To add additional colors without adding bulk to the entire piece, you can also insert small pieces of fabric under the cutout areas only, having the insert piece measure ½-inch larger than the opening all around.

3 Draw designs on the top layer.

4 Clip away the motif, taking care to cut *only* the top layer. (Keep the cutouts for possible use as appliqué patches once the reverse appliqué is completed.)

5 Turn under the raw edges of the cutouts slightly; pin, if necessary. You might instead find it helpful to apply a few drops of Liqui-Fuse along the turned-under edge. You can then fuse the edge under and stitch it to the lower layer more easily.

Quilter Jean Biddick uses the basic Mola reverse appliqué technique with Marcus Brothers' "Starburst" tie-dye-inspired fabric, finishing the appliqué edges with a simple machine blanket stitch.

6 Stitch, using a neat, invisible hemstitch.

7 Next, clip a smaller parallel shape in the second color; again be careful not to cut the layers beneath it.

8 Turn under edges as before and sew. Repeat for the remaining layers, except the last. As you turn under and stitch each layer, keep the widths of the visible areas consistent; the result should be several parallel bands of color, each echoing the cutouts of the top layer.

9 If desired, position the small cutout scraps on the piece and apply them as regular appliqués, turning under the edges and sewing with an invisible hemstitch.

10 To fill in any remaining gaps in the overall design, try adding hand or machine embroidery stitches in these areas.

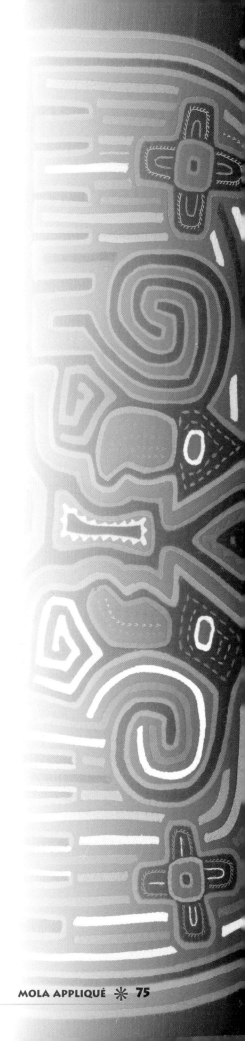

This pillow takes mola's solid color brights a step further, incorporating tie-dye-inspired prints from Marcus Brothers Textiles.

MOLA APPLIQUÉ PILLOW

Here, I was able to combine mola's traditional red and black color scheme with the interesting visual effects of a vibrant tie-dye fabric. The large 16-inch repeats of this particular tie-dye design were perfect for a decorative throw pillow.

I folded the top layer into squares, then into triangles, and made all cuts at once. This was a shortcut method to obtain a symmetrical design. And it gave the mola an interesting twist, providing a good example of how to borrow elements (mola colorations with tie-dye fabric) and blend them into a look that is uniquely your own.

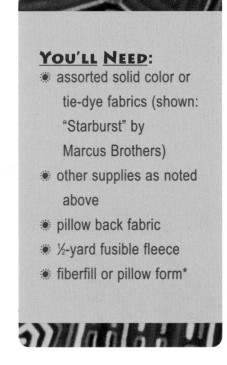

YOU'LL NEED:
* assorted solid color or tie-dye fabrics (shown: "Starburst" by Marcus Brothers)
* other supplies as noted above
* pillow back fabric
* ½-yard fusible fleece
* fiberfill or pillow form*

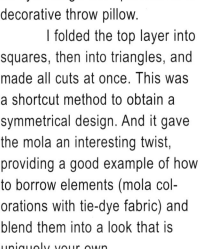

1 Instead of drawing individual motifs as described on the previous page, cut a square from large tie-dye print, centering one of the "bull's-eye" patterns.

2 Fold the square in half twice, then fold this square into triangles twice, as shown at right.

3 Make cuts into the folds, similar to cutting paper dolls or doilies. To test patterns, make practice cuts on paper first.

4 Layer the other fabric colors, then layer the top fabric.

5 Baste all layers together, and complete the mola as described in step 2 of the previous "Try Mola Appliqué" section, adding any additional appliqués and hand or machine embroidery stitches desired.

6 The size of the tie-dye repeat you originally cut will determine the finished size of the pillow. Cut pillow back fabric to the size of the mola.

7 Cut two squares of fusible fleece the same size as the pillow front, fusing fleece to the wrong sides of both the front and back of the pillow.

8 With right sides together, sew front to back, leaving an opening for stuffing.

9 Turn right-side out and press.

10 *Insert a pillow form if pillow is a standard size; otherwise, stuff with fiberfill.

11 Close the pillow opening with small hand stitches.

16" square and fold in half

Fold into 4   **Fold in half diagonally**

Folds

Cut designs and open

To reduce bulk, you can insert cuts of fabric large enough to cover the size of the cutout above it, rather than cutting complete squares of each fabric.

Sample Mola Appliqué Patterns

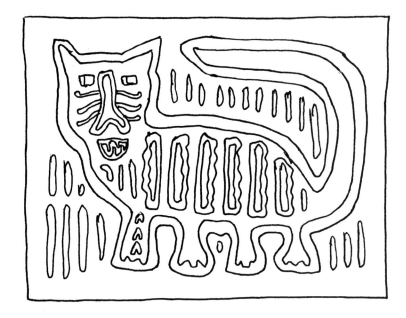

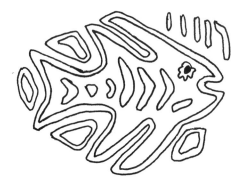

CHAPTER 8

BATIK
(INDONESIA)

A classic silk-screened Indonesian batik.

Photo courtesy Exotic Prints/Ady Jensen

THE TERM "BATIK" (pronounced ba-TEEK) is known in all regions of the world, referring to the process of applying wax to fabric so that the waxed areas resist the dyes, forming one-of-a-kind designs. *Batik* is an Indonesian-Malaysian word that originally described the dyeing and patterning process itself, but it is now used interchangeably to also refer to the finished fabric.

Indonesian methods and designs represent the highest form of artistic expression through batik, which allows fiber artists the freedom of hand-drawing their designs, compared to, for example, the creative restrictions of weaving designs into fabric. The process of completely immersing a fabric into the dyes also imparts a high level of durability and resistance to color fading.

Indonesian batik production can take three different forms, beginning with *tulis* batik, the oldest process. This method is named for the pen-like tool used to apply beeswax to the fabric, which is commonly stretched across a wooden frame. The tool, also referred to as a tjanting (pronounced CHAN-ting), is made of bamboo or wood, with a small copper container attached to it. The melted wax flows from the container through one or more small spouts, directly onto the fabric. The wax is kept nearby in a small pot with a flame beneath it, keeping it melted as the batik artist works. Some batik artists draw designs in the cloth first in pencil, but the most experienced apply the wax freehand. Once all wax is applied, the first dye is poured onto the fabric. Then, a second coat of wax is added to cover certain areas before the next dye color is applied.

Subsequent colors are added in the same way, and then the cloth is dipped in boiling water to melt the wax away. Artists apply the lightest colors first, working up to the darkest colors to be used in the design. Tulis batik is labor-intensive and traditionally made by women. A single cloth can take months to complete.

Copper stamp batik developed in the mid-1800s from a need to speed up and simplify the batik process, and is customarily done by men. Designs are embossed into a series of copper plates by metal artists to create the tjap (pronounced "chop"), or stamp. This faster, easier copper method results in regular repeats of the given motif, which lack the fluid look of the previous designs done by hand. The metal worker must duplicate the tjaps in mirror image in order to print both sides of fabrics used for sarongs. Some producers combine both tulis and copper stamping in a cloth to gain the benefits of each: fluid design plus faster production.

The most recent Indonesian batiks are made through a silkscreen process. Still hand-printed, silkscreened batiks offer beautiful quality that is produced relatively quickly at a reasonable price.

Java is the center of Indonesian batik production. Within Java are four regions, each with a particular batik style, explains Ady Jensen, authentic batik importer and owner of Exotic Prints. Each style is influenced by another region of the world, making batik a truly multicultural textile art.

Conventional batik production involved the use of a tjap to apply the wax to the fabric. Experienced artists create designs freehand.

Later, copper stamping was developed to make the batik process less time-consuming.

Ady Jensen, an importer and expert on Indonesian batiks, loves to promote the use of the fabrics in creative quilting projects.

Sarongs crafted in Cirebon feature the brighter colors and motifs of Chinese influence. Teal, yellow, and orange are not uncommon colors employed in this style.

Pekalongan styles are derived from Indo-European wallpaper patterns, including a very recognizable floral bouquet.

Batiks made in Yogyakarta are predominately indigo designs against light-colored backgrounds; the varying shades of blue set it apart from the rest.

Solo batiks are reminiscent of African prints, according to Jensen. These are known for their dark brown and nearly black motifs set against a gold-yellow, usually in a diagonally striped design.

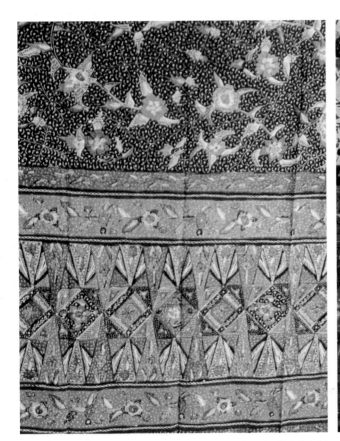

Batiks from the Cirebon region of Java are marked by their bright colors, a Chinese influence.

The symbolism involved in batik design can sometimes be difficult to decipher because one symbol can have numerous meanings, even within the same region. Most are drawn from nature. One commonly used motif is the *Garuda*, a representation of the man-eagle found in Hindu mythology and used by royalty. Garuda can be represented as a single wing (Lar), a pair of wings (Mirong), or a pair of wings joined at the center with a stylized, decorative tail (Sawat). These four symbols are common to all of the regions; however, there are many, many more that are only used in one village or another.

According to Jan Smiley, the original owner of Batiks, Etc., the high levels of artistry found in Indonesia's batiks can be attributed in part to the rich soils of the region. Requiring relatively little cultivation, the fertile land allows the people of Java, Bali, and surrounding islands more time for the mastery of creative pursuits. In addition to batik-making, Indonesian artists have earned a worldwide reputation for forged silver jewelry and carved artifacts of wood and stone.

The technique is believed to be more than two thousand years old, with some evidence pointing to early forms of batik in Africa, Asia, and the Middle East as far back as the third or fourth centuries. Neither the place nor date of its exact origin are confirmed, but it's a commonly held thought that batik was brought to Asia from the Indian subcontinent.

The craft was taken to Europe as a result of Dutch colonization of Java in the seventeenth century. There, the technique was imitated and mass-produced by European textile manufacturers, and later, it was applied to leather and paper as well.

Photo courtesy Exotic Prints/Ady Jensen

This pattern features indigo and soga dyes, common to Yogyakarta batiks.

Photo courtesy Exotic Prints/Ady Jensen

Depictions of Garuda, a man-eagle in Hindu mythology, include this double-winged style known as Mirong.

Wax batiks often give you two decorating options. Note the front, above, with clear greens at the top and bottom, and the rust tree trunk. Turn to the reverse for a darker design option, at left.

Batik is primarily used for clothing and accessories, especially the sarong, a popular wrap skirt style. To some extent, it is also used for such home furnishings as window treatments, tablecloths, napkins, and bed covers. At one time, fine batik fabrics were even used as currency.

The sought-after patterns are recreated in many different fabrics that are also commonly referred to as batiks, whether or not the fabrics are made with the true resist process.

DECORATING WITH INDONESIAN BATIK

Batik comes in so many colors, styles, and patterns that decorating options abound. You can easily display a collection throughout a room in various ways:

☀ Scenic batiks stretched over a wooden frame for quick but dramatic wall art.

☀ No-fuss slipcover simply tucked into sofa cushions for a fresh look. Wrap and tie coordinating patterns around throw pillows, or sew pillows as described below.

☀ Room divider screens; cut the batik into two or three vertical panels.

☀ Window treatments, from simple panels to roller shades to valances. (Remember to add a lining to help resist fading.)

☀ Table coverings.

☀ Bed canopies.

Create a decorative accent that's in keeping with the original and most well-known use of batik as sarong-style skirts and other wrapped garments by outfitting a decorative cloth doll in the fabric. This exotic lady, by doll designer and teacher E'dee Eubank-Robinson, shows off authentic silk-screened batik, with a small border design strategically placed along the edge of the sarong, and simply tied halter top.

A world collection of batiks might include Zimbabwean sadza as a quick sofa cover-up and the scenic wall art piece from West Africa.

"The Spirit from Within" by E'dee Eubank-Robinson pays tribute to batik's original use as sarongs and other simply styled wrap garments.

You'll Need:

* ☀ natural fiber fabric (cotton lawn or muslin, silk broadcloth, handkerchief linen, etc.)
* ☀ wax (candles, paraffin, beeswax, or batik wax)
* ☀ fabric dyes
* ☀ brown craft paper or clean newsprint
* ☀ double-boiler placed on an electric hot plate, or an electric glue pot
* ☀ iron
* ☀ kitchen thermometer

TRY BATIK!

Tjantings are available through specialty craft retailers and catalogs. For repeating designs, try cutting stencils from metal craft sheets to give the look of an Indonesian batik made with a tjap. Note that batik wax is simply a blend of paraffin and beeswax.

1 Melt wax, maintaining a consistent temperature of approximately 170 degrees.

2 Using the tjanting or stamp, create a design on the fabric. If you are making a multicolored design, only apply wax in areas where the first color will be resisted. Begin with the lightest colors first; be sure to cover these with wax as you add new colors.

3 For a crackle effect: Paraffin wax is the most brittle, so it gives the most visible effect, while other types are softer, giving a more subtle crackle. Cover the fabric thoroughly with wax and allow to cool. Crumple the fabric in your hands. This creates the cracks that the dye will seep through.

4 Prepare dyebath according the dye manufacturer's instructions.

5 When the wax has solidified and cooled completely, immerse the waxed design into the dyebath, or paint dye onto the fabric.

6 Apply wax again in the appropriate areas to resist the second color, let wax cool, and apply second dye color.

7 Repeat the process for any remaining colors in your design.

You'll Need:

(for Flanged Pillow,
12 by 16 inches):

- ☀ Indonesian batik cotton
- ☀ coordinating border fabric (metallic cotton was used in the sample)
- ☀ coordinating back fabric
- ☀ fusible fleece
- ☀ fiberfill
- ☀ accent beads
- ☀ scissors
- ☀ sewing machine
- ☀ thread
- ☀ iron

Indonesian batik lends itself to beadwork, quilting, trim embellishments, and other creative touches.

INDONESIAN BATIK PILLOWS

Study batik fabric for sections with specific motifs to "fussy-cut," and center on a pillow front. The designs in batik fabrics lend themselves to creative embellishments like quilting and beadwork. The vibrant royal blue pillow fabric was first hand-beaded and quilted by Ady Jensen.

FOR FLANGED PILLOW, 12 BY 16 INCHES

1 From batik, cut a rectangle measuring 9 by 14 inches.

2 Cut 3-inch-wide strips from the flange border fabric; then cut two lengths measuring 9 inches.

3 Sew strips to both short sides of the batik, right sides together, with a ½-inch seam allowance. Press seams toward batik.

*TIP:
Make the most of your batik yardage by using a simpler coordinating fabric for the back.*

Batik pillow fabric hand-quilted and hand-beaded by Ady Jensen.

4 Cut two more strips for the long sides, including the added length of the shorter flange sides.

5 Sew strips to batik, right sides together, with a ½-inch seam allowance. Press seams toward batik.

6 Cut backing fabric to the same size as the pillow front, including flange strips. Cut two pieces of fusible fleece the size of only the batik fabric, not including flange strips.

7 Fuse one piece to the wrong side of the batik; center the other piece over the wrong side of the backing fabric. Fuse both pieces.

8 Pin pillow back to pillow front, right sides together, and sew with a ½-inch seam allowance, leaving a 6- to 8-inch opening on one long side for turning. Turn; trim corners, and press.

9 Using a matching color thread, machine-stitch along the seams between the batik and the flange, leaving a 6- to 8-inch opening on one long side.

10 Evenly stuff pillow with fiberfill to desired firmness. Machine-sew the opening, using a zipper foot, or sew by hand. Hand-sew the opening at the edge of the pillow with small stitches.

11 Embellish pillow as desired with beads or other trims.

FOR TRIMMED PILLOW, 20 INCHES SQUARE

1 Fussy-cut a 15-inch square section of batik fabric to center a particular motif, adding ¾-inch hem allowance to all sides.

2 Turn under ¾-inch on each side and press. Hem with fusible tape or machine stitching.

3 Pin cording along the edge of the batik; baste in place.

4 From coordinating fabric, cut two squares 23½ inches each, and cut two fleece squares the same size. Fuse fleece to the wrong sides of the fabric squares.

5 Center the batik piece over the right side of one pillow piece, positioned as a diamond shape, and pin.

6 Using a zipper foot, sew around the batik fabric, stitching close to the piping.

7 Pin metallic trim to the pillow front, placing it ½-inch from the cording. Sew trim by hand or machine.

8 Pin pillow front to back, right sides together. Sew around all sides with a ¾-inch seam allowance, leaving a 12- to 15-inch opening for turning.

9 Turn; press. Insert pillow form, and close the opening with small hand-stitches.

YOU'LL NEED:

(for Trimmed Pillow, 20 inches square)

- ☀ Indonesian batik cotton
- ☀ coordinating fabric (linen was used in the sample)
- ☀ fusible hem tape
- ☀ fusible fleece
- ☀ 20-inch square pillow form
- ☀ 1½ yards each cording, metallic trims
- ☀ scissors
- ☀ sewing machine
- ☀ thread
- ☀ iron

WHILE TIE-AND-DYE techniques for patterning fabric appear in nearly every continent of the world, one distinctive style that stands out among the rest is Nigerian adire (pronounced ah-DEER-ay) cloth. More specifically, the term adire eleso refers to the Nigerian tied-and-dyed resist method, while adire eleko is the proper name for resist patterns created by the application of starch to the cloth before color is applied.

The story of adire eleso begins with Yoruba women, called *aladire*, who manipulate the fabrics, creating patterns that will appear once the fabric is dyed. They fold, stitch, pleat, and twist the fabric, securing it with raffia ties or thread. Tritik is a generic term used to describe designs formed by sewing the fabric. To achieve dots or circles in a pattern, small stones or seeds are tied into place (eleso literally means small stones or seeds).

Once patterns are secured, an indigo dye bath brings them to life. Indigo is the deep, rich blue dye derived from plants containing the coloring agent, indigotin. More than one type of plant carries the agent, which helps to explain the widespread use of indigo around the world. In Nigeria, the indigo-producing plants and the resulting dye are revered, since blue is one of the most significant colors used to honor the ancestors; one who dyes cloths, or an *aloro*, is believed to work under the protection of the Yoruba spirit *Iya Mapo*. After dipping the tied cloth into the indigo vat, often the aloro will dry the cloth thoroughly, then dip it once more after the resist ties and stitching are removed so that the contrast between dyed and undyed areas doesn't appear too great. This results in various shades of indigo within a piece.

The original method of adire eleso probably utilized locally handwoven cotton cloths like those used in other parts of West Africa. These are generally made of thicker cotton yarns that are

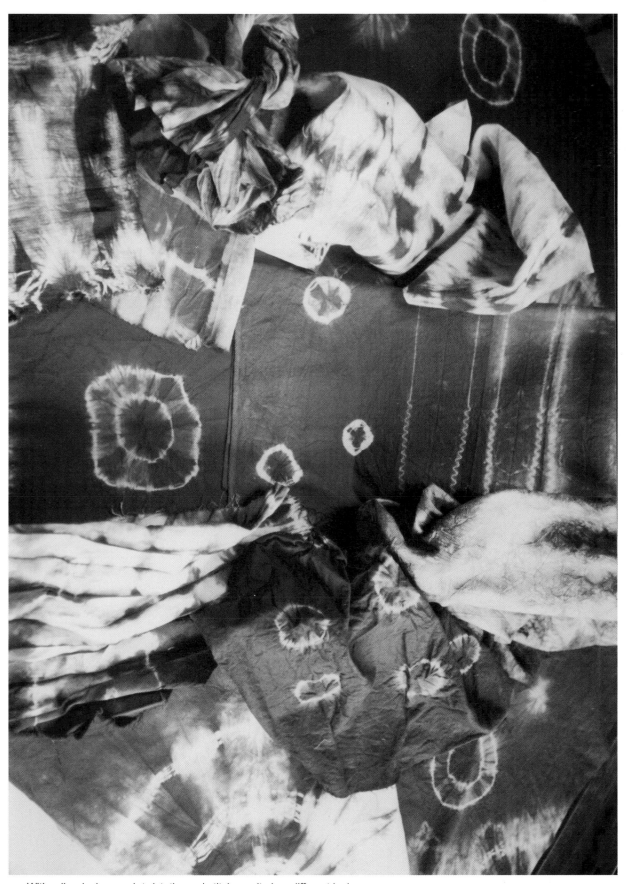

With adire dyeing, each twist, tie, and stitch results in a different look.

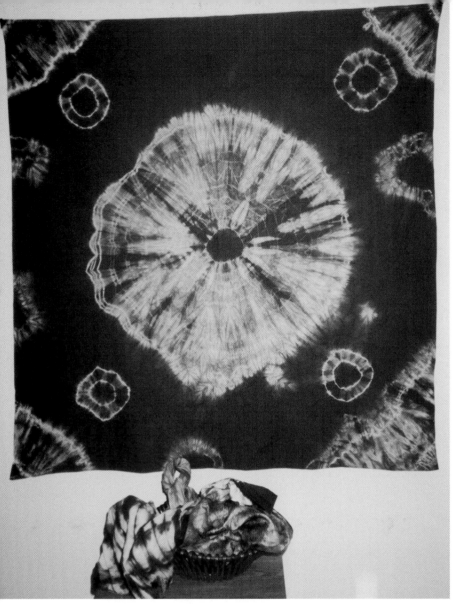

Adire cloths are versatile for home décor, and the effect is easy to recreate with basic fabric dye.

hand-spun, then handwoven on narrow looms. This adaptable fabric is used for a variety of textile arts including mudcloth from Mali and scenic korhogo panels from the Ivory Coast.

Later, in the 1920s and '30s, trade with European textile merchants brought forth a plentiful supply of cotton shirting fabrics. This new, lighter weight of the shirtings, as compared to the handwoven cottons, gave the aladire a completely different medium with which to create, as well as many new end uses. The increased quantities of plain fabric allowed them to more freely express their craft while simultaneously sharpening their entrepreneurial abilities. It was at this time that adire eleko developed, along with other lesser-used resist methods.

The emerging industry, centered in the Yoruba towns of Abeokuta and Ibadan, was still considered "the work of the ancestors," and even as production increased, the young women artists remained passionate and focused in their craft. Two cloths were stitched together to form a women's wrapper garment, and many of the designs were given names. Two patterns that became especially popular were *Olokun*, or "goddess of the sea," named for the Yoruba deity, and *Ibadadun*, which means "Ibadan is sweet." The prized indigo craft of the region attracted buyers from all over West Africa.

Those seeking adire tie-and-dye products would find Surulere in Lagos, Nigeria, a good place to find adire cloths as well as finished garments made from adire. Here, adire makers and dealers line the streets with an exciting mix of merchandise. Tailors are also situated here, ready to create custom garments almost on the spot, while some of the adire is instead prepared for export.

Photo courtesy the African Art Museum of the SMA Fathers, Tenafly, New Jersey

Similar indigo-based cloth patterning techniques are also used farther west, among the Wolof, the Snoike, and the Mandingo, and as far south as the Kasai region in the Democratic Republic of the Congo. Today, indigo is produced in India, China, Indonesia, South America, and Africa. In Japan, shibori is a spot-dyeing indigo technique with several variations around the country, applied to cotton as well as silk.

Here, stitches are ripped open to expose a striped adire pattern.

Tie-and-dye fabrics have also been found in nineteenth century Hungary, where resist patterns were created with pebbles, seeds, and grasses. In addition, tombs of the ancient Incas in Peru have turned up samples of tie-and-dye textile fragments dating back before the Spanish conquest in the fifteenth century.

Even the United States has a little-known history involving indigo. Before the American Revolution, indigo was one of the most

Photo courtesy the African Art Museum of the SMA Fathers, Tenafly, New Jersey

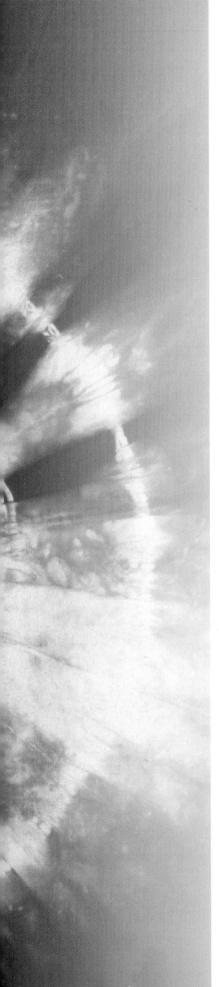

profitable crops, with South Carolina leading the colonies in indigo production. The plants thrived there not only because of slave labor, but also the vast knowledge of cultivation the West African captives carried with them. However, with the end of the Revolution, crop subsidies from England dried up, and indigo cultivation fell with it.

Today, a few pieces of adire would be a cherished addition to any fabricholic's collection. Adire is one of the less-accessible fabrics presented in this book, but it's well worth the effort to locate it. It's on my list of pieces-yet-to-acquire, either by my own travel or that of friends and associates, but until then, I've found that the simple do-it-yourself version is fun and still gets the point across—but only temporarily!

Even though the rich, distinctive indigo hues are what make adire what it is, in true Global Eclectic style, we're free to express our own version of the cloth, creating it to fit our style and décor, so another color can be substituted for what then becomes an "adire-inspired" look.

Decorating With Adire Eleso

The classic color combination of indigo with white lends itself to so many decorating styles and color schemes.

Adire's beauty also lies in its individuality, and patterns can be created to appeal to nearly any taste, whether you're after a homey, country farmhouse effect or furnishing a sophisticated urban brownstone.

The cloth speaks for itself, so simpler applications are best.

With adire, one piece is never enough to show the many possibilities of the craft; this makes it a perfect category for collectors. With that in mind, consider "group display" ideas, like several throw pillows showcasing various patterns or a table setting, as shown, with different patterns for the table cloth, napkins, centerpiece accent, etc. Another opportunity to show off a variety of patterns is to trim sets of navy bath and hand towels for a guest bedroom or powder room. Even a simple arrangement of adire cloths, casually tossed and spilling over the edge of a wicker basket, is a dramatic presentation for a coffee table, the top of a staircase, or any empty corner. Choose a small basket for a table top, or a larger rattan accent urn that might otherwise be used for long twigs, bamboo sticks, etc.

A stunning mix of adire cloths is used to dress a dining table, paired with placemats done in mudcloth for contrast.

Adire is a versatile cloth, so I prefer to decorate with it in unstructured ways as mentioned above. In a given week, the same cloth can be used as a dining room table drape, hallway wall hanging, living room sofa throw or mock slipcover—even a skirt or headwrap! It's the ultimate fabric alternative for the Global Eclectic decorator who loves to change the look of a room at a moment's notice.

You'll Need:

* natural fiber fabric, plain weave (cotton broadcloth and muslin, and silk douppioni were used in these samples)
* fabric dye (such as RIT or Tintex) in navy, indigo, denim blue, or similar color
* rubber bands, string (bakery-box type), twine
* large stainless steel pot
* stove top or hotplate
* sink for rinsing the fabric
* wooden spoon or stick
* rubber gloves
* liquid laundry detergent
* sewing machine, thread for stitched patterns (optional)

Here, you can see the detail of the adire fabric as used for the sofa cover shown on page 93.

TRY ADIRE ELESO!

It's fun to simply experiment to achieve a variety of patterns, but if you have a particular use in mind, you can think ahead about what areas to tie off. If desired, cut several pieces of fabric about 9 by 12 inches, and tie each one differently to test the resulting patterns before dyeing your final cloth. Remember that even with testing, duplicating an exact pattern can be difficult, but this is the beauty of handcrafted textiles.

1 Dissolve dye in hot water, following the manufacturer's instructions. Stir regularly.

2 Meanwhile, begin to tie off the patterns in the fabric. The tighter you bind each section of fabric, the better the resist will show up; make looser ties for more subtle patterns, or tighter ties for more contrast between the dyed areas and those that remain the original fabric color.

Consider any one of the following variations:
a. Rings and random circle patterns: Pinch a section of fabric and bind tightly with a rubber band. For a sunburst effect, add additional rubber bands below the first, spacing these the distance you want the rings to appear.
b. Twist patterns: Subtle contrasts result, since the fabric is only tightly bound at the ends. Twist the entire fabric length into a rope until it curls over itself. Bring ends together and bind with a rubber band.
c. Stripe patterns: Pleat the fabric in accordion folds, then fold the fabric in half lengthwise. Band tightly with rubber bands approximately every 2 inches.
d. Marble patterns: Gives an acid-wash effect that is fairly consistent throughout the fabric. Scrunch fabric up into a ball, distributing the fullness evenly. Randomly tie fabric strips or bakery-box string around the bundle, crossing over it in every direction. The binding should be taut, but not extremely tight.

3 Continue to stir the dye. Keep it on a low, consistent heat to maintain a slow simmer, but well below boiling point.

4 Thoroughly wet the tied fabrics with warm water. This helps them to accept the dye more readily.

5 Immerse the fabrics into the dye, making sure they are completely covered. Stir slowly and regularly.

6 After ten to fifteen minutes, remove fabrics, squeezing out the excess dye back into the pot. (Note that deeper color can be produced with a longer soaking time. Some samples were left in the dye bath up to 30 minutes, with great results.)

7 Add a small amount of liquid detergent to each fabric bundle, rinsing it out under warm running water. Gradually change the running water to cool, then cold, until the water runs clear and free of blue dye.

8 Squeeze out excess water; remove ties. Marvel at the artistry!

9 Machine dry or air dry. Press.

NOTE: To lessen the high contrast of white and blue areas, you can re-dip the cloth, giving the white a light blue appearance instead. Holding it at the corners, immerse the cloth fully (or just the desired areas), and pull it back out of the dye bath in one smooth, continuous motion, squeeze out excess water, dry, and press.

For more gradual color adjustments, you can also lighten the dye first. Place some dye into a second container and dilute with water, then re-dip the cloth once or as needed. Squeeze out excess water, machine or air dry, and press. Refer to the dye manufacturer's instructions for fabric care.

Adire's most basic designs are achieved through tying off small sections to create rings (left), twisting fabric into ropes (right) for a less defined, overall tie-dye effect, and pleated and bound (top) for striping effects.

TIP: Wearing rubber gloves is recommended while working with the dye.

The medium shades of blue suggest that this fabric was redipped, to lessen the contrast of stark white with dark blue, and the remaining threads show that the stripes were achieved by stitching.

ADIRE TABLE ACCENTS

Set a dining table bursting with West African flair, by pairing adire cloths with contrasting tasseled placemats in mudcloth. (The placemat instructions are in *African Accents*, page 57.)

The square table cover was tied and dyed to achieve a larger central design as well as corner accents. As with any tie-and-dye project, the designs in each corner vary a bit, but together, they present a uniform look. Add stability to the lightweight cotton adire with fusible interfacing.

Then, use very different tie patterns for each napkin for a fun and unique touch. I designed these with fusibles for "no-sew" ease, but you can also machine machine-sew, if desired.

1 From the adire cloths, choose one for the table cover and trim it to the desired finished size, plus 1 inch all around.

2 Turn under 1 inch along each end of the table cover fabric; press.

3 Following the manufacturer's instructions, test the interfacing by fusing a piece (at least 6 inches square) to the fabric. Let cool, then evaluate the interfacing's effect on the fabric. If you prefer a firmer hand, fuse a second piece of interfacing right on top of the first. Cut interfacing to measure ½-inch smaller all around than the table cover. Be sure to cut straight, using sharp scissors or a rotary cutter.

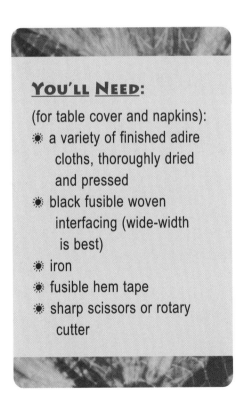

YOU'LL NEED:

(for table cover and napkins):
* a variety of finished adire cloths, thoroughly dried and pressed
* black fusible woven interfacing (wide-width is best)
* iron
* fusible hem tape
* sharp scissors or rotary cutter

Bendable craft wire can be shaped into napkin rings, a great final touch.

4 With the wrong side of the table cover up, center the interfacing over the fabric. Fuse interfacing to fabric. Give the table cover a final press from the right side.

5 For each napkin, cut a 17-inch square. Turn under ½-inch on all sides of the napkin; press.

6 On one side, open up the fold and position a length of fusible hem tape between the fold. Fuse hem in place. Continue around the remaining sides of each napkin. The crisp edge formed by the fusible tape gives the napkin added body for your own creative folding styles. (This bond is designed to be permanent; if the hem releases after laundering, it usually means that the nakpin was not fused long enough originally. Simply re-fuse it.)

7 Leftover adire pieces can be arranged to spill out of a vase or other decorative container, as an attractive and conversational alternative to flowers.

COLLECTING BY COLOR

Is **THERE A COLOR** that you never get tired of, one that stops you in your tracks every time, whether it's a suit someone is wearing or a car that just drove past? Or maybe you just find yourself collecting paint chips and fabric swatches featuring this color, regardless of the fabric design. When asked what your favorite color is, do you find it impossible to give a one-word answer?

If any of these scenarios sound familiar, then that color is probably a great collectible theme for you.

This is part of my collection of dark reds. I've been drawn to

The color you're passionate about is the perfect place to start your global eclectic treasure hunt, or to fine-tune your existing collection.

this color family for years and have incorporated it into several rooms in the house. For me, it's a very earthy, relaxing, and inviting color. Since these are smaller accent pieces and fabrics, the effect is never overpowering. This group represents a wide range of reds, but nothing bright or glaring; it's mostly muted, darker tones, and some even faded or antiqued. Pimento, brick, clay, rose, Indian red, Chinese red, raisin, claret, oxblood, paprika, chili, cinnabar, and rust are descriptive color names for the pieces in this collection. I've even bought and

Here, shades of turquoise and blue predominate in this cozy sofa throw. It's made of fabrics collected on various trips over the years. Again, it includes a variety of shades in the turquoise family, ranging from greens to blues, providing the perfect lift for an otherwise neutral décor. By collecting fabrics within a particular color story, you can later create an easy patchwork sofa throw. Each time you travel, visit fabric stores with this project in mind, and the resulting patchwork becomes a tangible reminder of your adventures.

framed greeting cards that pass my "dark red test," and maybe you've noticed the most prominent color on the cover of *African Accents* . . .

One easy way to pull together pieces for "Global Eclectic" décor is to work with your particular color, a plan that is especially effective if you're starting out with a versatile, fairly neutral color palette in furniture, rugs, and other basics. By varying the shades and intensities of your chosen color, and varying the objects as well, you'll end up with an interesting mix of pieces that work, whether you keep them together or scatter them throughout your home. Even better, they're interchangeable from room to room. It's also easy to add new pieces, knowing that they will fit into your very personalized decorating scheme.

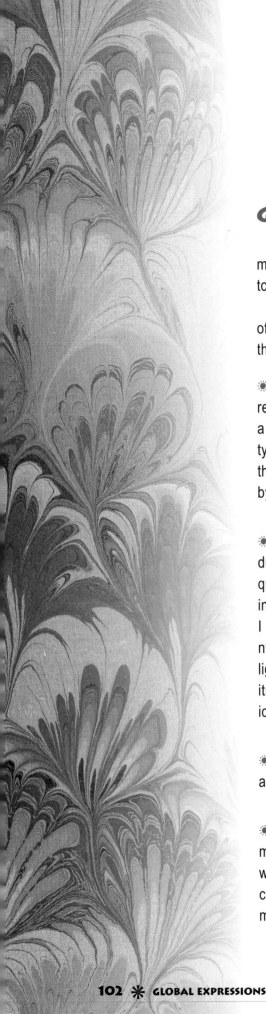

SHOPPING FOR SPECIAL TEXTILES

GLOBETROTTER TIPS

Traveling and shopping naturally go hand-in-hand. Just as I mentioned in the opening pages of *Global Expressions*, the best way to acquire your fabric collection is firsthand, by traveling the world!

These are a few thoughts and ideas to help make the most of your shopping excursion, whether it's across continents or across the country:

❋ Before your trip, have some idea of what the specialties of the region are, such as kente strip weaving in Ghana. Sometimes, when a country is known for a particular textile art, varying grades of quality are offered to satisfy the average tourist's taste and budget, while the "better" grades and finer antique fabrics might be harder to come by, as described in the chapter on mola art, for instance.

❋ Pack lightly when you go, and include a couple of empty folded duffels in your case, secure in the knowledge that you'll fill them quickly for your return trip. Or, try packing your clothes and belongings in one suitcase, then place that into a larger suitcase. In 1994, I traveled to Hong Kong with other fabricholics, returning with a filled nylon duffel bag of nearly 30 new fabric acquisitions. The large but lightweight nylon bag weighed nothing on the way there and served its purpose perfectly! (Remember to bring extra luggage locks and identification tags for these extra bags.)

❋ Consider carrying small but useful items such as a tape measure and a calculator for figuring exchange rates easily.

❋ If you're shopping for a rug or other large item, bring measurements of the floor, wall space, or other area to be covered. Likewise, when color-matching is important, visit your local paint store and choose a few paint chip swatches; bring these along to help you make the best selections while shopping.

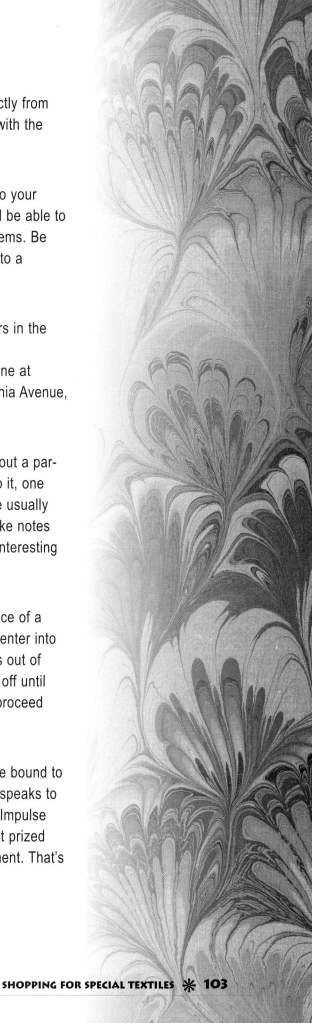

☀ Lucky enough to be purchasing something special directly from the artisan? Ask for permission to photograph him or her with the piece, adding to its "history."

☀ Look into your options for shipping merchandise back to your home. A hotel concierge or local shipping company should be able to provide typical shipping and insurance costs for various items. Be sure any quotes cover delivery fees *to your door*, not just to a Customs clearing agent.

☀ Customs regulations are another consideration: Readers in the United States can get a copy of "Know Before You Go," a publication of the U.S. Customs Service. It's available online at www.customs.gov/travel, or by writing to: 1300 Pennsylvania Avenue, Washington, DC 20229.

☀ Take advantage of any opportunity to ask questions about a particular piece. There's often an interesting story attached to it, one you'll want to share when you return home. Merchants are usually happy to share this information with visitors. Be sure to take notes because as much as you think you'll remember the most interesting details, you might not.

☀ Understand that in some cultures, simply asking the price of a fabric or other artifact can be regarded as an invitation to enter into bargaining negotiations. It's best to avoid asking for prices out of mere curiosity; this can be considered rude. Instead, hold off until you find pieces you would seriously consider buying and proceed from there.

☀ Remember that even with research and planning, you're bound to come across an art form you know nothing about, but if it speaks to you and is within your budget, don't be afraid to act on it. Impulse buys aren't always a bad thing and often become our most prized possessions, partly because of the excitement of the moment. That's what world travel is about!

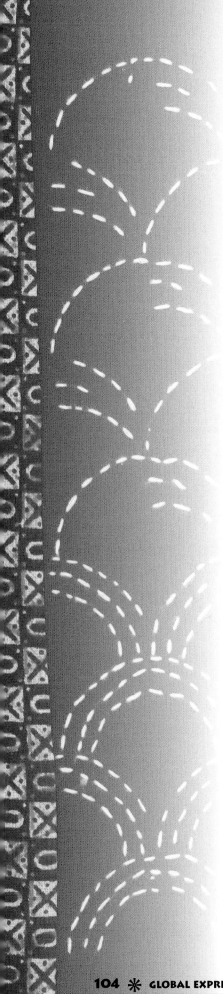

CARING FOR SPECIAL TEXTILES

SPECIAL TEXTILES have existed with little or no interference from us for thousands of years, but it's still helpful to keep in mind a few simple guidelines. Whether you spend a lot on your world fabric stash or a little, it's easy to give them the attention they deserve, allowing you to enjoy their natural beauty and positive energies for years to come:

☀ Collectible fabrics are obviously best kept in a **smoke-free home**. Remember this when bidding on online auctions for something you can't touch—or smell—before you buy. You can usually ask sellers questions via e-mail before you bid. Smoke-free storage should be at the top of your list of questions.

☀ **Direct light** is one the greatest threats to any fabric, especially a collectible one. Ultraviolet (UV) radiation is the most damaging, found in natural daylight as well as florescent bulbs. While these cause the quickest damage, exposure to full-spectrum, or regular incandescent lighting, is also detrimental to fabrics over time, contributing to color fading and brittle fibers. Lessen these effects by regularly rotating the fabrics you display to limit their light exposure. A seasonal, or four-month, rotation is recommended by the Textile Museum in Washington, D.C. Display a fabric for four months, then store it for the rest of the year. *Not only will this help to protect your investment, but such professional advice is the perfect justification for continually growing your collection, too!*

☀ **Proper storage** can't be over-estimated. It's important to refold stored fabrics regularly, to avoid permanent creasing in any one section of the cloth. Another option is to roll up textiles for storage, especially larger pieces like quilts and floor coverings. Acid-free papers, boxes, and rolling tubes can be a worthwhile investment for serious collectors. Generally, attics and basements are *not* recommended as storage areas. A better choice is a cool, dry bedroom closet, or other area within the main living space of your home, where room temperatures are not subject to hot or cold extremes.

☀ **New acquisitions** should be carefully inspected before they are brought into your home for the first time. Dust, dirt, and insects can be removed by gently beating the piece outdoors. Regular vacuuming should also be a part of your seasonal display turnover, before fabrics are again placed into storage. Use a low-power, handheld vacuum for best results.

☀ **General handling** tips include washing your hands first to remove any traces of lotions, perfumes, or natural body oils that might transfer to the fabric. Likewise, remove your rings and other jewelry to prevent snagging loose threads.

FABRIC RESOURCES AND CRAFT SUPPLIES

THE SOURCES LISTED below are where you'll find some of the authentic textiles discussed in Global Expressions, as well as suppliers whose products were used in creating both the do-it-yourself versions of the fabric and the finished projects:

SADZA BATIKS

Shambakodzi Crafts
Contact: Mollin Madziwa
e-mail: shambakodzi@hotmail.com
Cooperative representing the works of Zimbabwean textile artists as well as other craft producers.

Novica.com
11835 West Olympic Boulevard
Suite 750E
Los Angeles, CA 90064
(877) 2-NOVICA
Learn about the lives and works of artisans from around the world and shop a wide variety of "Global Eclectic" merchandise.
Novica.com promotes more than 1,700 artisans worldwide, where artists set their own prices and receive individual recognition for their talents. Features Kudhinda Fabrics, potato-stamped textile products like pillows, etc.

Zimports
384 Vermillion Avenue
St. George, UT 84790
www.zimports.com • sales@zimports.com
(800) 653-3857
Importers of sadza batiks, Shona stone sculptures, and other art from Zimbabwe; wholesale and retail.

TAPA CLOTHS

Malcolm Finaulahi Dreaneen
e-mail: malcolmd@monotapu.com
www.monotapu.com
Exports a variety of authentic Tongan tapa cloths and other
Polynesian crafts to individual and wholesale customers worldwide.

MARBLED FABRICS

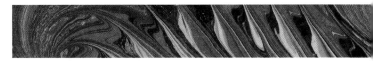

Marbled Fabrics by Marjorie Lee Bevis
www.marbledfabrics.com
Sells beautifully marbled cottons and silks as fabric for crafts and
quilting, and as finished fashion accessories (scarves, neckties, etc.)
Classes and helpful hints are also offered on the site.

INDONESIAN BATIKS

Exotic Prints
Ady Jensen, Owner
918 Tropical Lane
Key Largo, FL 33037
Phone and Fax: (305) 451-5676
Importer of Indonesian batiks. Jensen has an extensive background
in the fabrics, from the methods used to their historical and cultural
significance, practical usages, silk-screening, and more.

ADIRE

Adire African Textiles
www.adire.clara.net
This informative Web site has adire and other authentic African fabrics for purchase. Run by Duncan Clark, author of *The Art of African
Textiles*.

CRAFT AND TEXTILE SUPPLIES

(used in the book)

Beacon Adhesives/Signature Crafts
P.O. Box 427
Wyckoff, NJ 07481
(800) 865-7238
Liqui-Fuse liquid fusible web.

Brother Sewing Machine
100 Somerset Corporate Boulevard
Bridgewater, NJ 08807-0911
(800) 4-A-BROTHER
www.brother.com
Sewing machines.

Delta Technical Coatings
2550 Pellissier Place
Whittier, CA 90601
(800) 423-4135
www.deltacrafts.com
Acrylic paints, finishes and media for decorating fabrics and general crafts, including **MarbleThix instant marbling kit**.

Dollversity.com
P.O. Box 39557
Redford, MI 48239
(800) 949-4236
e-mail: dollversity@hotmail.com
www.dollversity.com
This site offers **dollmaking kits**, supplies, and classes. E'dee Eubank-Robinson, the designer of *The Spirit from Within*, likes to "bring the diversity of dollmaking to appeal to the child in all of us."

Eastwind Art

P.O. Box 811

Sebastapol, CA 95473

(707) 829-3536

www.eastwindart.com

An excellent source for authentic **sashiko supplies**, from fabrics to threads and needles. Also carries patterns for Japanese-inspired home décor, crafts, and apparel.

Home Arts

1979 Falcon Ridge Drive

Petaluma, CA 94954

(888) 639-8570

High-quality **cardboard kits**, ready to cover with fabric, including tissue boxes, picture frames, and desk accessories.

HTC, Inc.

103 Eisenhower Parkway

Roseland, NJ 07068

www.htc-inc.net

Fusible craft products, including fusible fleece and the Fuse-A-Shade Fabric Roller Shade Kit.

International Fabric Collection

3445 West Lake Road

Erie, PA 16505

(800) 462-3891

www.intfab.com

Carries **sashiko supplies** and an outstanding selection of fabrics from around the world; a great line of related books, patterns, notions, and more for international textile enthusiasts. Call for showroom hours and appointments and look for IFC at various shows and expos around the country (a schedule is also on the Web site).

Liquitex Artist Materials
P.O. Box 1396
Piscataway, NJ 08855-1396
(800) 445-4278
www.liquitex.com
A leading source for **artist paints, mediums, and finishes**; also **bendable craft wire** (page 99). Supplies for textile painting, marbling, and other techniques. Web site also includes projects and helpful hints for using the products.

Marcus Brothers Textiles, Inc.
980 Avenue of the Americas
New York, NY 10018
info@marcusbrothers.com
www.marcusbrothers.com
Extensive line of high-quality **craft and quilting fabrics** from traditional and country to contemporary and ethnic-inspired collections.

Putnam Company, Inc.
P.O. Box 310
Walworth, WI 53184
(800) 338-4776
www.putnamcoinc.com
Pillow forms, as well as Special Edition **fiberfill for ethnic doll designs** (available in black, brown, and caramel, as well as standard white).

RIT Consumer Affairs
P.O. Box 21070
Indianapolis, IN 46221-1070
(317) 231-8044
www.bestfoods.com
Fabric dyes and treatments (Navy Blue #30 and Denim Blue #36 used for the adire cloth).

Speedball Art
P.O. Box 5157
Statesville, NC 28687
(704) 838-1475
www.speedballart.com
Tools and supplies for **block printing**.

Stemmer House Publishers, Inc.
2627 Caves Road
Owings Mills, MD 21117
(410) 363-8459
www.stemmer.com
Produces design books, with **copyright-free, reproducible** designs
suitable for fabric crafts, including the International Design Library,
a culturally diverse collection of books that are affordable and easy
to use.

Viking Sewing Machine Co.
31000 Viking Parkway
Westlake, OH 44145
(440) 808-6550
www.husqvarnaviking.com
Designer 1 computerized sewing machine.

Complementary pieces from my dark reds collection: Indian heavy embroidery (left),
Kuba appliqué cloth from Central Africa (top), and a newer acquisition, block-printed
fabric from India (foreground).

GENERAL RESOURCES

HERE YOU'LL FIND museums, Web sites, books, and other interesting resources for further study and enjoyment of world textiles, over and above those already mentioned. Learn more about the fabrics, cultures, and general textile-related techniques for home decorating.

The African Art Museum of the SMA Fathers

23 Bliss Avenue
Tenafly, NJ 07670
(201) 541-1280
A well-rounded collection, housed on the grounds of the SMA Church, which includes textiles, masks, pottery, and other objects. Call for information on upcoming exhibits and special events.

Batik Butik
953 Kentwood Terrace
Victoria, BC V8Y 1A5
CANADA
(250) 658-2612
www.batikbutik.com
Imports mostly rayon batiks from Bali.

Batiks Etcetera
200-B West Main Street
Wytheville, VA 24382
(800) 228-4573
www.batiks.com
Imported batiks, batik-inspired fabrics, and other world fabrics in cotton and rayon for fashion, quilting, and home décor.

Costume and Textile Collections at FIT
Fashion Institute of Technology
7th Avenue @ 27th Street
New York, NY 10001
(212) 217-7700
Extensive research and study materials for students and museum members, including swatch books.

Craft World Tours – CWT
6776 Warboys Road
Byron, NY 14422
(716) 548-2667
A variety of tours focusing on handcrafts and textile arts from around the world.

Dharma Trading
Box 150916
San Rafael, CA 94915
Catalog of supplies for textile artists.

Djema Imports
70 West 125th Street
New York, NY 10027
(212) 289-3872
www.djemaimports.com
Another personal favorite for mudcloth, African cotton prints, korhogo, brocade and more. Sells wholesale and retail.

Earth Henna
Lakaye Mendhi Studio
1800 North Highland Avenue
Suite 316
Hollywood, CA 90028
(323) 460-7333
www.earthhenna.com
Mendhi body painting supplies and a book with designs adaptable to Indian block printing.

Earth Tones by Aisha Kureishy
(217) 877-7168
e-mail: aisharukh@home.com
Fine embroideries and novelty fabrics imported from Pakistan.

eBay.com
Online auction. Fun to shop, with new people to meet.

Fabritique
84 East Plain Street
Wayland, MA 01778
(508) 545-1617
e-mail: fabritique@att.net
www.fabritique.com
"Beautiful fabric from faraway places."

Galen Berry's MarbleArt Supplies
2462 NW 38th Street
Oklahoma City, OK 73112
(405) 949-1239
http://members.aol.com/marbling/marbling
Hand-marbled papers and marbling supplies.

Interweave Press
www.interweave.com
(800) 272-2193
Publishes books and magazines about fiber arts, including Piecework.

Just Africa Gallery
(508) 775-0448
www.justafrica.com
African artifacts for home décor.

Kaarta Imports & Exports
121 West 125th Street
New York, NY 10027
(212) 866-5190
One of my favorite shopping spots has a huge variety of African cotton prints, along with mudcloth, korhogo and other African fabrics. Sells wholesale and retail.

Kerr Grabowski
www.kerrgrabowski.com
A fiber artist with a contemporary twist on Indian block printing techniques. Offers workshops and lectures.

Leo9 Textiles
1906 Miriam Avenue
Austin, TX 78722
(512) 472-1655
e-mail: leo9@texas.net
Importers of Australian Aboriginal cotton prints as well as sarong-length batik cottons from the island of Java in Indonesia.

Maiwa Handprints
#6, 1666 Johnston Street
Granville Island
Vancouver, BC V6H 3S2
(606) 669-3939
www.maiwa.com
Retail store and studio offers workshops in all kinds of fiber arts, plus authentic tools and supplies for various world textile arts.

MarbleArts Studio
e-mail: marble@nccw.net
http://members.nccw.net/marble/index.html
Contemporary marblers in the Italian tradition.

The Museum for Textiles
55 Centre Avenue
Toronto, Ontario M5G 2H5 Canada
(416) 599-5321
www.museumfortextiles.on.ca

Quilters' Express to Japan
80 East 11th Street, #623
New York, NY 10003
(212) 505-0480
Offers high-end Japanese fabrics for quilting and fashion sewing via club membership.

QuiltEthnic.com
Interesting resources are listed here for quilting with influences from African, Asian, Indian, Hawaiian, Aboriginal Australian, and other unique traditions. Lots of information and great links are shared.

Saidou's African Art
Saidou Ceesay, Owner
(718) 992-6140
Specializing in mudcloth, kuba cloths, Indian embroideries, wall hangings, and novelty embroidered and beaded pillow covers.

St. Theresa Textile Trove
1329 Main Street
Cincinnati, OH 45210
(513) 333-0399
e-mail: sttheresatextile@aol.com
www.sttheresatextile.com
Carries a great selection of fabrics with a global focus, plus trims, beads, findings, etc.

The Textile Museum
2320 S Street NW
Washington, DC 20008-4088
(202) 667-0441
www.textilemuseum.org
Interesting collections and an in-depth offering of textile books.
Special events are scheduled year-round, and the Learning
Center is a great resource for fabric lovers of any age.

Treadleart
25834 Narbonne Avenue
Lomita, CA 90717
(310) 534-5122
www.treadleart.com
All kinds of supplies for sewing, quilting, and general needle arts,
including sashiko needles and threads, and shisha mirrors for
Indian embroidery work.

Tribal to the Max
215 North Rodney Street
Helena, MT 59601
www.tribalmax.com
A cool resource I discovered while shopping eBay for artifacts.

The Unique Spool
407 Corte Majorca
Vacaville, CA 95688
www.uniquespool.com
Interesting, imported fabric prints from world resources; also patterns and books.

GLOSSARY

Abstract - A design that is free-form, not representative of any particular object.

Acquisition - A prized addition to a collection, such as a museum acquisition, or a special piece added to one's personal grouping of home furnishing collectibles, such as textiles, masks, carvings, etc.

Adire eleso - An indigo tie-and-dye method of fabric decoration from Nigeria, West Africa.

Adire eleko - A starch-resist method of indigo dyeing from Nigeria.

Aladire - A Yoruba woman who ties and stitches cloth in preparation for indigo dyeing.

Aloro - One who holds the special position in Yoruba culture of dyeing adire cloths in Nigeria.

Alum - A chemical used as a pre-treatment for fabrics prior to marbling to make the designs permanent instantly. Also called aluminum sulfate.

Appliqué - A method of fabric embellishment where small pieces of fabric are sewn to the surface of a base fabric to form pictures or decorative designs.

Batik - A resist technique for applying color and pattern to fabric, usually by way of wax. Found around the world in varying forms, but associated most with Indonesia. The term has become generic to describe any fabric that resembles the technique, even mass-produced look-alikes.

Block printing - A process of transferring dyes and pigments to fabric with carved wood or linoleum to create repetitive designs.

Buttonhole twist - A very heavy machine sewing thread, used to create a more visible outline around appliqués or trapunto designs.

Carragheenan - A fine, powdered extract of dried seaweed (Irish moss) that thickens water sufficiently to allow paints to be floated and manipulated on the water's surface for marbling. Also a common thickening agent used in processed foods.

Cooperative - An organization of artists who work together to promote and sell their creations. Education, marketing, and increasing public exposure to the crafts are usually the primary goals of its members.

Diameter - The measurement across the widest part of a circle.

Distress - To give paper or fabric a beaten, weathered, or aged look by dampening, wrinkling, and then drying it.

Dowel - A solid wooden tube used for craft projects, available in various thicknesses from ⅛-inch and larger.

Ebru - The original Turkish word for marbling, meaning "cloud art."

Embroidery - A method of decorating fabric by hand- or machine-stitching it with contrasting thread, usually heavier types, such as embroidery floss, buttonhole twist, metallic threads, Perle cotton, or other novelty threads.

Flange - A flat fabric border added to the edges of a pillow; can be of contrasting fabric or the pillow fabric itself.

Fusible - A no-sew craft product that is applied to fabric with the heat of an iron. When a fusible is bonded to a fabric, the bond is meant to be permanent.

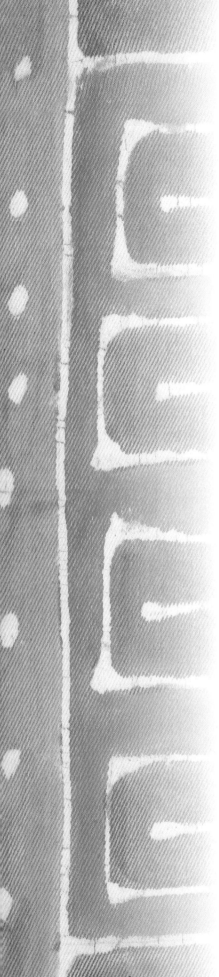

Fusible craft backing - A layer of nonwoven material that stabilizes the project. It is ironed to the wrong side of a fabric. Available in various weights, including heavier-weight window roller shade backing.

Fusible fleece - Craft padding (approximately ¼-inch thick) with fusible web applied to one side. Can be used for picture frames, pillow linings, quilts, etc.

Fusible web - A thin, random web of glue placed between two layers of fabric to join them with the heat of an iron, instead of sewing. The paper-backed version allows you to apply the web to one fabric first, peel the paper away, and then iron this fabric to the second one. The paper protects your iron from contact with the sticky web. Unlike fusible craft backing that remains a third layer in the project, fusible web melts into the fabric layers, disappearing as it bonds them. Also available as a tape.

Fussy-cut - Selecting and cutting out a particular motif or design from a fabric print in order to center it, for instance, on a pillow front, or as an appliqué on a quilt.

Global Eclectic - A term to describe an emerging home decorating style that includes artifacts from many world cultures, artfully blended together for a unique look.

Gujarat - A leading region in India for block-printed textiles and other art forms.

Hari Kuyo - An annual ceremony in Japan where needle artists collect their broken and used needles, paying tribute to them, and praying for continued creative skills for the coming year.

Indigenous - Originating in, growing in, or naturally occurring in a particular environment, such as the tree barks used to make tapa cloth or plants required to make certain pigments.

Indigo - The dyestuff derived from various plants found around the world that contain the pigment indigotin, creating a rich blue color. Most notably used in Nigerian adire cloth and Japanese sashiko.

Influence - A borrowed element from a particular culture, such as a color, motif, or artistic technique, incorporated into a project to create a new version or usage.

Kuna - Native people of the San Blas Islands, off the Caribbean coast of Panama. Kuna women produce mola reverse appliqué work.

Mamanu - Samoan tapa cloth that is painted with natural dyes in the customary way, as compared to upeti rub-off designs.

Mendhi - An ancient body art of temporary tattoos, practiced in the Middle East, Africa, and India. Many mendhi designs are similar in style to Indian block printing motifs.

Mola - An intricate cutwork technique of the Kuna Indians. Kuna women create unique reverse appliqué with bright colors and extensive hand-stitching.

Mon - Japanese family crests designs that are adapted and stitched into sashiko patterns.

Monotone - A fabric or other artwork that features a single color, or possibly varying shades of that one color.

Motif - A design, shape, or symbol used to decorate a textile or other object.

Ngatu - The Tongan term for tapa cloth after it has been decorated.

Particle board - Strong but lightweight wood product used in crafting. Found in the lumber department of home improvement centers.

Perle cotton - A soft, twisted thread used for Sashiko stitching, embroidery, and other needlecrafts.

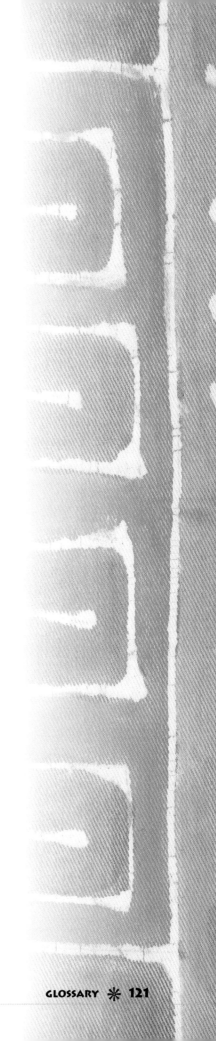

Pigment - A dye or coloring, usually derived from plants, berries, or other natural sources.

Plexiglas - Acrylic plastic sheeting used for crafting as well as inexpensive replacements for glass windows.

Registration - The degree to which a stamped design repeat matches up to the previously stamped image, creating an unbroken, continuous design; a measure of the fabric-maker's skills and significant to the value of the finished piece.

Resist - A method used to prevent dyes or pigments from penetrating certain areas of a fabric. Resists can be wax or starch-based, or can be achieved through tying or stitching fabrics before color is added.

Right sides together - A basic sewing term describing a seam joining two pieces of fabric, where the right sides of the fabric face each other as they are stitched.

Rites of passage - Cultural ceremonies or events that mark milestones in one's life, such as the transition from childhood to adulthood.

Rub-off - A method of transferring a pattern from one surface to another, used in some tapa cloths from the South Pacific. Also used to transfer patterns from a book, whereby a symbol is photocopied from the book, the back is rubbed with a lead pencil, and the sheet is placed right-side up over the fabric or other surface. The symbol is traced over, leaving a pencil lead tracing on the fabric, to then be painted or otherwise decorated.

Sashiko - A Japanese quilting method, usually small, even, white stitches worked against indigo blue fabric in exact and repeating patterns. Originally used to reinforce work garments.

Sadza - A cornmeal resist batik method form Zimbabwe. Also the food that is a staple of the Zimbabwean diet.

Shisha mirrors - Small mirrors about the size of a dime, used as one of many embellishments in Indian embroideries. Mirrors are held in place with crochet-like stitches in heavy threads.

Shona - A South African people of Zimbabwe. Shona artists are widely known for sadza batiks, potato-stamped fabrics, and their smooth, stylized stone sculptures.

Saipo - The term used in Samoa to describe tapa cloth.

Stylized - A design whose elements represent the artist's view of a particular object, not necessarily a realistic image of the object as it really appears. An incorporation of the artist's own "style."

Suminagashi - A Japanese form of marbling on paper. Inks are gently blown across the water to achieve delicate patterns on the paper.

Tapa - A nonwoven textile formed from inner tree bark, it is pounded and decorated; primarily found in the Pacific Islands.

Textile medium - A liquid that is added to craft paints when used on fabrics to help them penetrate more readily and increase washability.

Tjanting - A tool used to apply wax to fabric by hand in tulis batik-making.

Tjap - The carved copper stamps commonly used in Indonesian batik-making.

Tonga - An island in the South Pacific, known as the top producer of tapa cloth.

Trapunto - A wholecloth quilting method featuring raised and stuffed areas to create interest. Believed to have developed in Italy as a measure of wealth among the aristocracy.

Tulis - The original style of Indonesian batik, named for the pen-like tool used to apply the melted wax to the fabric.

Upeti - The rub-off version of tapa cloth produced primarily in Samoa.

Wholecloth - A quilting variety that employs one full-sized piece of fabric, as in trapunto quilting, compared to quilt tops made from many small fabric pieces sewn together.

Block-printed fabrics make dramatic bedroom accents.

BIBLIOGRAPHY

Andrew, Dolores M. *Italian Renaissance Textile Designs*. Maryland: Stemmer House Publishers, Inc., 1986.

Bosense, Susan. *Hand Block Printing & Resist Dyeing*. New York: Arco Publishing Co., 1985.

Caraway, Caren. *The Mola Design Book*. Maryland: Stemmer House Publishers, Inc., 1981.

Cohen, Paula and Daniel. *Marbling on Fabric*. Colorado: Interweave Press, 1990.

Corbin, George A. *Native Arts of North America, Africa, and the South Pacific*. New York: Harper & Row Publishers, 1988.

Dendel, Esther Warner. *African Fabric Crafts*. New York: Taplinger Publishing Co., 1974.

Gillow, John and Sentance, Bryan. *A Visual Guide to World Textiles*. London: Thames & Hudson, Ltd., 1999.

Gillow, John and Barnard, Nicholas. *Traditional Indian Textiles*. London: Thames and Hudson, Ltd., 1991.

Keller, Ila. *Batik – The Art and Craft*. Charles E. Tuttle & Co.

Lyton, Linda. "The Mirror Work of Gujarat," *Piecework*, November/December 1994.

Maile, Anne. *Tie and Dye As A Present Day Craft*. New York: Ballantine Books, 1963.

Matsunaga, Karen Kim. *Japanese Country Quilting: Sashiko Patterns and Projects for Beginners*. Tokyo and New York: Kodansha International, Ltd., 1990.

Newman, Thelma. *Contemporary African Arts and Crafts.* New York: Crown Publishers, 1974.

Newman, Thelma R. *Quilting, Patchwork, Appliqué and Trapunto: Traditional Methods and Original Designs.* New York: Crown Publishers, 1974.

Pritchard, Mary J. *Saipo: Bark Cloth Art of the Samoa.* American Samoa Council on Culture, Arts and Humanities, 1984.

Singer, Margo and Spryou, Mary. *Textile Arts: Multicultural Traditions.* London: A & C Black, Ltd. 1989.

Singer Sewing Reference Library. *Fabric Artistry.* Minnesota: Cowles Creative Publishing, 1998.

Soltow, Willow Ann. "Molas and their Makers," *Piecework,* November/December 1994.

Storey, Joyce. *The Thames and Hudson Manual of Textile Printing.* London: Thames and Hudson, 1974.

Tana, Pradumna and Rosalba. *Traditional Chikankari Embroidery Patterns of India.* Maryland: Stemmer House Publishers, Inc., 1988.

Victoria and Albert Museum. *Batiks.* London: Crown Publishing, 1969.

ALSO BY LISA SHEPARD

African Accents: Fabrics and Crafts to Decorate Your Home, published by Krause Publications (October 1999), inspires and guides readers in the use of authentic African textiles for home decorating, incorporating them in more than 40 fun and practical projects.

An introductory chapter explains the origins and cultural significance of **mudcloth**, **korhogo**, **adinkra**, **kente**, and **kuba raffia fabrics**, and chapters that follow cover the living room, dining area, home office, master bedroom, child's room, and entertaining accessories. Extensive resource and supply listings guide readers in recreating the projects in the book and encourage further study and enjoyment.

African Accents was awarded the Craftrends 2001 Award of Excellence in the Quilting and Sewing Books category. In a market dominated by country and "traditional" home dec fabrications featuring florals, checks, and stripes, the book offers a fresh alternative for expressive home décor. It attracts anyone with an overall interest in ethnic design, at a time when eclectic, multicultural influences are especially strong for decorating. Around the world, African fabrics and the looks inspired by them have been featured in home décor, and *African Accents* is the first book to address the trend within the creative sewing and craft market.

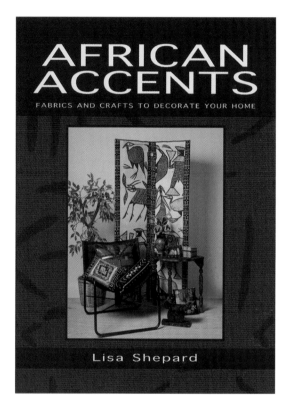

For more information:
visit: www.**CulturedExpressions**.com
e-mail: lisa@CulturedExpressions.com
write: Cultured Expressions
     P.O. Box 3643
     Union, NJ 07083

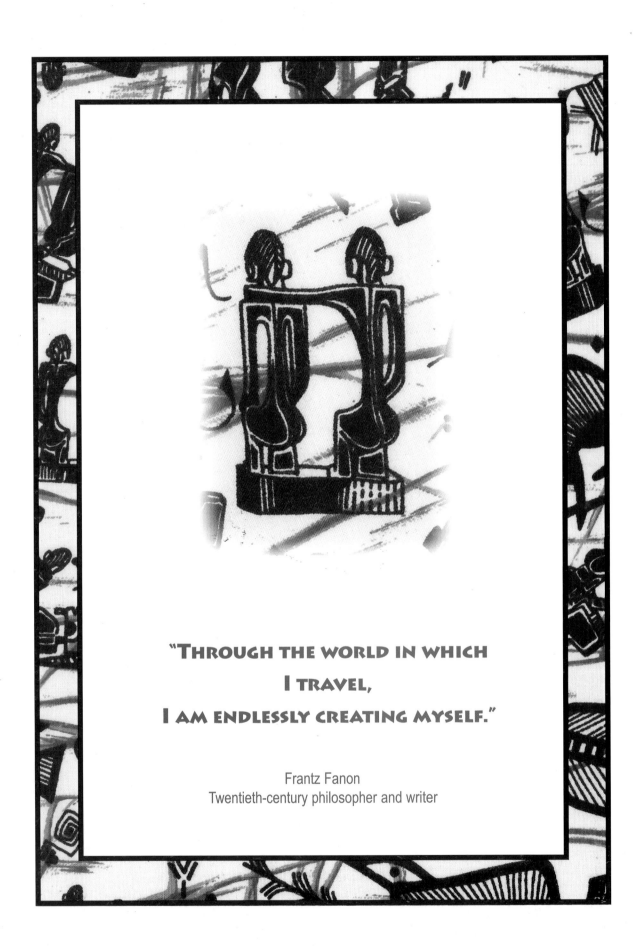

"THROUGH THE WORLD IN WHICH
I TRAVEL,
I AM ENDLESSLY CREATING MYSELF."

Frantz Fanon
Twentieth-century philosopher and writer